This book is brought to you by:

hackneyandjones.com

Writers and Publishers of
fiction and non-fiction.

Scan QR Code

Copyright © 2024 by Hackney and Jones. All rights reserved.

No part of this book may be reproduced in any form or by any electronic or mechanical means, including information storage and retrieval systems, without written permission from the authors, except for the use of brief quotations in a book review.

CONTENTS

INTRODUCTION: EMBARK ON YOUR ADVENTURE!		1
PART 1: GENERATING IDEAS — WHERE IT ALL BEGINS...!	GENRE	21
	SETTING	28
	THEMES	36
	EMOTIONS	46
	OTHER WAYS TO GENERATE IDEAS	53
	YOUR CHARACTERS	74
	TITLES	86
	COLOURS, NUMBERS, SHAPES AND DAYS OF THE WEEK	99

CONTENTS

	REPETITION AND THE RULE OF 3	107
	GOALS, OBSTACLES AND CONSEQUENCES	112
	THE INCITING EVENT	121
	PLOT TWISTS AND ENDINGS	124
PART 2: WRITING YOUR STORY	WRITING YOUR STORY STRUCTURE	130
	THE CONTENT: LANGUAGE — SATPIN	138
	PHONICS	142
	ALLITERATION	145
	ONOMATOPOEIA	148
	SIMILES	156

CONTENTS

	THE CONTENT: LANGUAGE	PATTERNED LANGUAGE	164
		RHYME	168
PART 2: WRITING YOUR STORY	SECRETS TO PAGE TURNERS		173
	SHOW, NOT TELL		177
	WRITING YOUR STORY		192
	EDITING YOUR STORY		198
PART 3: CREATING YOUR STORY BOOK	FRONT COVERS		204
	LAYOUT		207
	PUBLISHING		209
	YOUR CHECKLIST		211
RESOURCE TOOLKIT			214

INTRODUCTION

EMBARK ON YOUR ADVENTURE!

INTRODUCTION

WHY ARE YOU HERE?

We are assuming you are here because you want to write amazing children's stories, right? Maybe you have tried lots of things before or maybe this is your introduction to children's story writing.

Either way, welcome!

THE AIM OF THIS WORKBOOK?

This workbook aims to take you from a blank page to a fully written children's story, step by step, and to enjoy it along the way.

It is a streamlined roadmap to creating an awesome children's story from scratch – with never seen before techniques. We know this because we invented them!

Sound good?

THIS WORKBOOK IS MADE UP OF THREE PARTS

1- The teaching – so you know what you're doing and why.

2- The writing – how to structure your children's story and what elements of language to include.

3- The creation – how to get a front cover designed, what layout to use, and how to get published.

INTRODUCTION

WHY WE ARE DIFFERENT

We have read books about creative writing, taken courses etc. but found them far too 'fluffy'.

We wanted actionable steps. Can you relate?

So this workbook GIVES YOU the actual content and ideas so that you have inspiration at every step, rather than leaving you to come up with things yourself - ensuring zero writer's block!

THESE ARE THE VITAL ELEMENTS FOR YOUR CHILDREN'S STORY:

- Characters - Are they interesting? Will your readers enjoy reading about them?
- Settings - Where does your story take place? In the city? Space? In the country
- Plot - The sequence of events in your story to drive it forward.
- Goal - What does your main character want/need to achieve and why?
- Conflict - What/Who stands in your main characters' way of getting what they want?
- Consequences - What happens if your main character doesn't get what they want?

INTRODUCTION

IF YOU ONLY REMEMBER THREE THINGS BY THE END OF THIS PROCESS

- Your reader comes first – always. Make sure you create a children's story that keeps your young readers guessing, but one that's not too complicated. They (and the parents/carers) are investing time, energy and sometimes money reading your work. Don't worry – we've got you covered with EVERYTHING! Just follow the steps.

- Follow the roadmap we give you, but don't be afraid to create your own tracks as well. We personally advise outlining your stories - it really helps with writer's block - but when you are confident with the plot/scenes etc. don't be afraid to follow your inspiration.

OUR MOTTO FOR AVOIDING WRITER'S BLOCK

IF YOU CAN...

Use your imagination: Think of an awesome character from your imagination.

IF YOU CAN'T...

Use your observation: Think of a character you have read in a book or seen in the movies.

IF YOU NEED...

Resources: Use the resources section at the back of this workbook for inspiration.

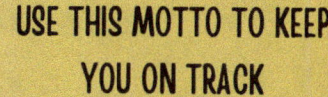

USE THIS MOTTO TO KEEP YOU ON TRACK

WHO ARE WE?

Hi, I'm Claire Hackney and I am a former teacher turned full-time novelist and publisher from Cheshire, England. My background in teaching English, Drama, and Media Studies fuels my storytelling passion.

My intrigue for history finds a home in my work, particularly in our 1950s-inspired novels (Meet Me at 10 etc.). Beyond this, I'm set to embark on an exciting path, including finishing the upcoming DI Rachel Morrison crime thriller series. My first children's book, 'Katie and the Kite,' was released in 2024.

Find me at:

TWITTER: @ClaireHac
INSTAGRAM: @clairehackneyauthor
WEBSITE: hackneyandjones.com

Hi, I'm Vicky Jones and I'm from Essex, England. I joined the Royal Navy at 20 but felt something was missing. So, I decided to make a bold list of 300 things to do, and my life transformed, especially after attending a writing group to help me write a novel which went on to become a bestseller.

I have also written songs for iTunes and YouTube. One of my songs, "House of Cards," is centred around the theme of bullying. I also co-wrote 'Meet Me at 10' with Claire, a book which deals with controversial societal issues.

I love to travel and have been to around 50 countries - so far! I have also also gained a psychology and criminology degree from The Open University.

Although now living in Cheshire, I keep ties with my Essex roots.

My journey is all about being creative, brave, and discovering myself.

My first children's book, 'Katie and the Kite,' was released in 2024.

Find me at:

TWITTER: @VickyJones7
INSTAGRAM: @vickytjones
WEBSITE: hackneyandjones.com

OUR WRITING JOURNEY

WE HAVE WRITTEN FICTION AND NON-FICTION BOOKS!

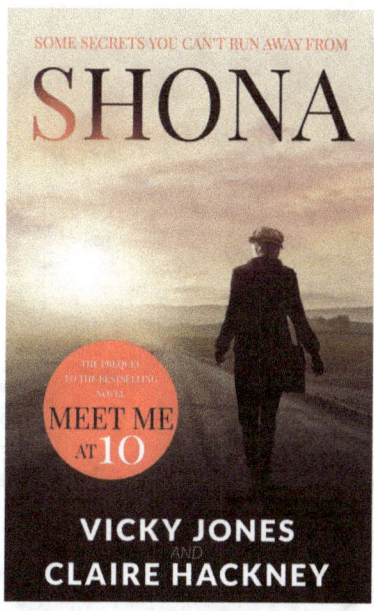
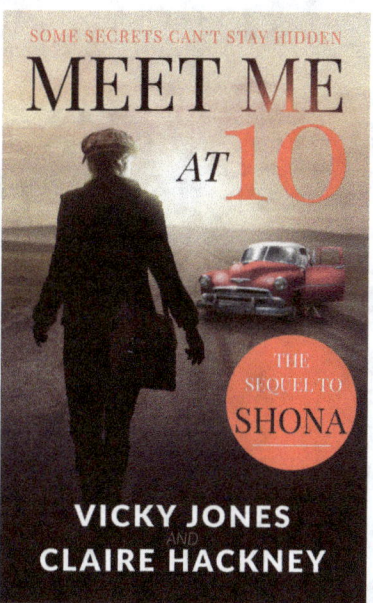

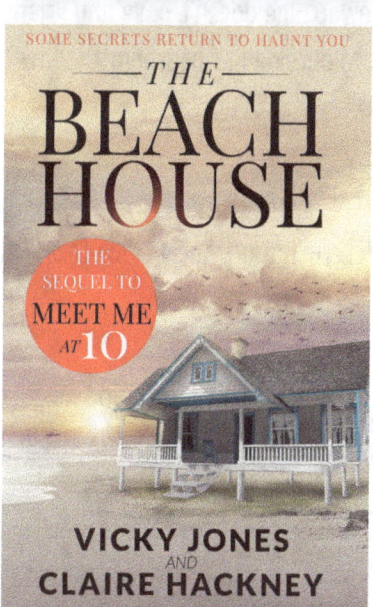

OUR EXPERIENCE IN WRITING CHILDREN'S STORIES

WE HAVE ALSO WRITTEN OUR OWN EARLY YEARS CHILDREN'S BOOK

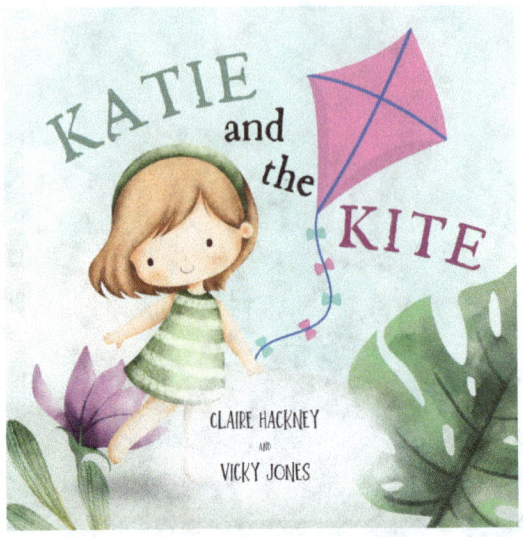

A beautifully heart-warming story teaching your child about resilience, courage and being a good friend. They will discover how small acts of kindness can go a long, long way.

Katie has moved to a new town far, far away. She doesn't have any friends yet and is longing to feel included. One morning, she hears a mysterious sound outside her bedroom window.

What could it be?

With a sense of curiosity, courage and determination, Katie finds friendship in the most unexpected of ways! Get ready for a story that'll make your heart soar!

Perfect for parents reading a bedtime tale filled with warmth and magic or for teachers to use for discussion on topics such as kindness, sharing, resilience, determination and friendship.

SCAN HERE

HOW TO BE A GREAT CHILDREN'S AUTHOR

To be a good storyteller you need to get in touch with your inner child.

THIS IS VERY IMPORTANT.

You need to try to see the world through the eyes of a child.

If you 'think' like an adult, and 'write like an adult,' your story will be only appropriate for adults.

MYTH BUSTING

MYTH	TRUTH
Writing children's stories is easy.	Crafting impactful children's stories takes practice. Writing concisely while conveying emotions and themes can be challenging.
I need to be an excellent writer.	You don't need qualifications to be a writer. You don't need to have 'done well at school.' If you're worried about spelling, grammar etc. software etc. can help with that.
Only published authors are "real" writers.	If you write, you're a writer. Publication isn't the only measure of success.
Writing children's stories has no impact.	Children's stories can evoke emotions, explore themes, and leave lasting impressions.
Picture books are so easy to write!	Picture books may seem simple to write, but there is a complexity, a structure, and a formula for a good story to make it good enough for a child to enjoy.
Writing children's stories is not "serious" writing.	Children's stories are respected literature. They pack a punch.
You need a degree in writing to be good at it.	Passion and willingness to learn matter more.
You must be original in every aspect.	Uniqueness comes from your perspective and voice.

Remember: Writing is a journey. Embrace your love for writing, be persistent, and trust in your ability to create meaningful stories.

THE BENEFITS OF CHILDREN'S STORIES AND PICTURE BOOKS

- They can bring families together and help children's vocabulary.

- It can create a bond at bedtime for parents/carers and their child.

- They can help soothe children to sleep.

- It can be picture book stories that introduce children to language and sounds.

- They can spark a child's imagination.

Globally, picture books outsell adult titles.

Children are CRAVING stories!

The industry isn't saturated by any means.

Picture books are the oldest form of storytelling. Think of cave paintings.

They are picture books on a wall.

THE BENEFITS OF CHILDREN'S STORIES AND PICTURE BOOKS

Picture books are a child's introduction to language and art. They can help them start learning about sounds, numbers, shapes, emotions etc.

Picture books can help children cope with emotion and challenging events in their lives such as the death of a parent or grandparent.

Even using (appropriate) humour can help with complex feelings

Be careful though -

AVOID using innuendo. You want both adults and children to be laughing at the same thing.

The whole story doesn't have to be funny, it can be sad at times. But children or animals being naughty will always go down well in stories.

Some picture books are text-heavy, and some are picture-heavy.

Some invite parents and children to answer questions and have a discussion about certain topics or themes.

Stories can be both educational and entertaining.

FAMOUS CHILDREN'S STORIES AND WHY THEY ARE POPULAR

"The Gruffalo" by Julia Donaldson –

'The Gruffalo' tells the story of a clever mouse who outwits various predators by inventing a fearsome creature called the Gruffalo. It is loved for its humourous rhymes, engaging plot, and memorable characters.

"The Tale of Peter Rabbit" by Beatrix Potter –

This story follows the mischievous adventures of Peter Rabbit as he sneaks into Mr. McGregor's garden against his mother's warnings. Its charming illustrations and timeless tale of curiosity and consequence have captivated readers for generations.

"The Very Hungry Caterpillar" by Eric Carle –

This story follows the journey of a caterpillar as it eats its way through various foods before transforming into a butterfly. It is loved for its colourful collage-style illustrations and simple, repetitive text.

WHERE COULD WRITING CHILDREN'S STORIES TAKE YOU?

Publication: Your children's story could be published by traditional or self-publishing routes, reaching young readers worldwide.

Recognition and awards: Exceptional stories may win awards, boosting your credibility and opening doors to more opportunities.

Adaptation: Successful stories may be adapted into movies, TV shows, or other media, expanding your story's reach and impact.

Educational use: Your story might be used in schools and educational programmes to promote literacy and learning.

Speaking engagements: You could be invited to speak at schools and events, inspiring young readers and fellow writers.

Workshops and teaching: Share your expertise by leading workshops on children's storytelling.

Merchandising: Popular characters could lead to merchandise opportunities, generating additional income.

Translations and global reach: Your story might be translated into multiple languages, reaching a diverse audience worldwide.

Impact on young minds: Shape young minds with your stories, instilling values and fostering a love for reading.

Personal fulfilment: Ultimately, writing children's stories can bring personal satisfaction, knowing you've entertained and inspired young readers.

WHAT HAS STOPPED YOU BEFORE?

There is a reason why you are here. Something has stopped you from either starting your story or writing 'The End,' right?

It is useful to know what those reasons are so you can progress.

Here are the most common reasons writers struggle. We will help you solve them all:

- Self-doubt:

  - Issue: Many new writers grapple with self-doubt, questioning their abilities and fearing that their writing won't meet their own or others' expectations.
  - Impact: This can lead to hesitation, perfectionism, and a reluctance to begin or complete a story.

- Overwhelm:

  - Issue: The sheer scope of writing a story, with its characters, plot, and settings, can be overwhelming for new writers.
  - Impact: Feeling overwhelmed can result in procrastination and a sense of being unable to navigate the complexities of storytelling.

- Lack of structure or planning:

  - Issue: Some new writers may dive into writing without a clear plan or structure, leading to uncertainty and difficulty in maintaining a coherent narrative.
  - Impact: Without a roadmap, writers may get lost or discouraged during the writing process.

- Fear of failure or criticism:

  - Issue: The fear of failure or criticism can be paralysing for new writers. The thought of negative feedback or rejection can hinder creative expression.
  - Impact: Writers may be hesitant to take risks, experiment with their writing, or submit their work for fear of judgment.

WHAT HAS STOPPED YOU BEFORE?

- Time management challenges:

  - Issue: Balancing writing with other responsibilities, such as work or studies, can be challenging for new writers.
  - Impact: Limited time may result in sporadic writing habits, making it difficult to maintain momentum and complete a story.

- The blank page:

  - Issue: Confronting a blank page can be intimidating, and the pressure to start with the perfect sentence can be paralysing.
  - Impact: The blank page challenge can stifle creativity and prevent writers from taking the initial steps in their storytelling journey.

- Confidence:

  - Issue: A lack of confidence in one's writing abilities can hinder the creative process, making it difficult to express ideas with conviction.
  - Impact: Low confidence may lead to second-guessing, self-censorship, and reluctance to share one's writing with others. Building confidence is crucial for a writer's growth.

Put simply...

- You won't write a whole story, you will write a scene, then another and then another.

- You will join them together and they just happen to create an engaging story!

- We take all the stress and overwhelm out of the process, so relax and enjoy!

THINGS TO AVOID

- Waffling – Every word must count, as you have to "get to the good bit" quicker than in longer-form stories.

- Word count for children's picture books tends to be around 100-600 words; sometimes more, sometimes less. There will be 1000 words at the most.

- Sexism, classism, racism, dangerous situations that kids may copy, scary scenes, horror, gore, drugs, sex, rude words, and offensive words must be avoided in your story.

All pretty basic, right?

WHAT THE BESTSELLERS DO

If a book is a bestseller, it means it is popular, right?

If it is popular on Amazon then more than a few people like it, would that be fair to say?

If we study the similarities between the top 5 bestsellers, we will AUTOMATICALLY know what readers want.

Always remember...

Your reader comes first. Why?

If your book/story isn't what they want, they won't buy it, or like it, and may leave a 1-star review on something like Amazon.

Emulate the best but DO NOT COPY them - this is important!

You want inspiration and information.

THE PURPOSE

If we know the similarities between popular picture books, with regards to storylines, front cover, characters, number of pages, types of illustrations etc., then we are on the right path to success.

We know if we included even a couple of those elements, our story could be a winner!

The bestsellers are giving you a treasure map to success.

There's no need to 'see' if something works, we have the answers right in front of us.

WHAT THE BESTSELLERS DO

Go to Amazon.

Type in the search bar: 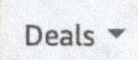 childrens picture books ages 3-5 years

Look at what comes up.

You want to avoid the 'sponsored' results – they are ads and are not there organically.

These are the results....

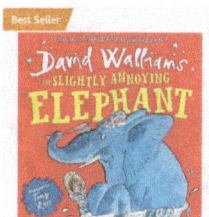 **The Slightly Annoying Elephant**
French edition | by David Walliams and Tony Ross | 7 May 2015
★★★★☆ ~4,060
Paperback　　　　　　　　　　　Ages: 3 - 5 years, from customers
£3.49 RRP: £7.99
✓prime One-Day
FREE delivery Tomorrow
More buying choices
£0.59 (39 used & new offers)
Kindle Edition

 **The Koala Who Could**
by Rachel Bright and Jim Field | 9 Feb 2017
★★★★★ ~6,739
Paperback　　　　　　　　　　　Ages: 2 - 5 years, from customers
£3.99 RRP: £7.99
Save 5% on any 4 qualifying items
✓prime One-Day
FREE delivery Tomorrow
More buying choices
£1.00 (35 used & new offers)

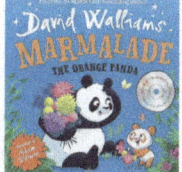 **Marmalade: The heart-warming and funny illustrated children's picture book from number-one bestselling author David Walliams!**
by David Walliams and Adam Stower | 11 May 2023
★★★★★ ~834
Paperback　　　　　　　　　　　Ages: 2 - 5 years, from customers
£6.00 RRP: £8.99
Save 5% on any 4 qualifying items
✓prime One-Day
FREE delivery Tomorrow

 **It's OK to be Different: A Children's Picture Book About Diversity and Kindness**
by Sharon Purtill and Sujata Saha | 19 Sept 2019
★★★★☆ ~5,775
Paperback　　　　　　　　　　　Ages: 2 - 5 years, from customers
£8.99
Save 5% on any 4 qualifying items
✓prime
FREE delivery Friday
Only 2 left in stock.
More buying choices

Ok, so now what?

 **We're Going on an Egg Hunt: A Lift-the-Flap Adventure (The Bunny Adventures)**
by Martha Mumford and Laura Hughes | 25 Feb 2016
★★★★★ ~3,218
Paperback　　　　　　　　　　　Ages: 1 - 3 years, from customers
£5.00 RRP: £7.99
Save 5% on any 4 qualifying items
✓prime One-Day
FREE delivery Tomorrow
More buying choices
£1.00 (32 used & new offers)

Let's see if they have anything in common at all and list these elements...

WHAT THE BESTSELLERS DO

Front covers: Colourful/bright

Main characters: Animals on the cover (apart from one)

Titles: Ask questions 'The Koala Who Could' (Do what?), 'The Slightly Annoying Elephant' (why annoying?), 'Marmalade the Orange Panda' (Why orange?)

Themes: Difference, courage, adventure

Font: Nice and big, easy to read, child-friendly font.

Being aware of the following will make your story popular with readers.

Front covers: Colourful/bright. I will design my cover to include ....

Main characters: Animals on the cover. I will include .... on my front cover.

Titles: Ask questions. My story title could ask the question ....

Themes: Difference, courage, adventure. My theme could include ....

Font: Nice and big, easy to read, child-friendly font. I will use the font .... in my story.

Just by filling in the above, your story will be so much better than other beginners as they will not have used this method.

You are meeting the demand of your target market and giving them stories they are actively looking for.

This equals SUCCESS!

PART 1

GENERATING IDEAS

WHERE IT ALL BEGINS...!

GENRE

GENRE

In writing, 'genre' refers to different categories or types of stories, like mystery, romance, fantasy, or science fiction.

It helps readers know what kind of story they're getting into.

The most popular genres for children's stories are:

Fantasy: Stories with magical elements, mythical creatures, and imaginary worlds.

Adventure: Exciting tales of characters going on quests, exploring new places, or facing challenges.

Fairy Tales: Classic stories with magical elements, often involving princes, princesses, witches, and talking animals.

Mystery: Stories where characters solve puzzles, uncover secrets, or unravel mysteries.

Animal stories: Tales where animals are the main characters, often with human-like traits and adventures.

Science Fiction: Stories set in the future or involving advanced technology, space exploration, or futuristic societies.

Humour: Funny stories that make children laugh, often with silly characters and playful situations.

Picture books: Stories accompanied by illustrations, aimed at younger children to help them understand and enjoy the story.

WHY IS IT BENEFICIAL TO WRITE IN A GENRE?

Connect with young readers: Following genre rules ensures that children can relate to the story and characters, enhancing their engagement.

For example, in a fantasy story, children might connect with magical creatures and enchanted worlds.

Provide familiarity and comfort: Genres offer familiar story structures and themes that children enjoy, making them feel comfortable and drawn into the story.

For instance, in a classic fairy tale, children encounter familiar elements like princes, princesses, and 'happy-ever-after' endings.

Teach lessons effectively: Different genres offer unique opportunities to convey important lessons or moral messages in a way that resonates with children, making the learning experience more impactful.

For instance, in a mystery story, children learn problem-solving skills and the importance of perseverance as they follow the protagonist's journey to uncover secrets and solve puzzles.

WHAT HAPPENS IF YOU DON'T USE A GENRE?

Writing without a genre in mind can result in a story lacking clear direction or style, making it harder for readers to engage with.

Example: Imagine a story that jumps between fantasy elements and mystery without committing to either genre, confusing readers about the storyline and expectations.

HOW TO PICK A GENRE

Firstly, think about what you are most excited about writing about.

Is it:

- a Space Adventure story?

- a Fantasy type story?

- Set in Space

- Set underwater

- Featuring animals

- Nature etc.

STILL NOT SURE?

We call this our Resource Toolkit.

We have done all the research for you.

All you have to do is look through the collection of ideas in each genre and then pick your favourite!

Head to the Resource Toolkit section on page 214 and see which type of genre you would like to write in.

HOW TO PICK A GENRE

THINK:

Which cover are you MOST drawn to?

What type of story are you interested in?

WHAT NOT TO DO WITH WRITING GENRES

- Don't mix different types of stories that don't go together, like putting pirates in a space adventure, especially for your first story. Keep it simple.

Example: Combining a historical romance with elements of science fiction.

- Avoid ignoring the typical elements or rules of your chosen genre, as it might confuse readers.

Example: Writing a mystery without any clues or suspense.

- Avoid trying to force your story into a genre it doesn't naturally fit into, as it might feel forced or unnatural.

Example: Trying to turn a comedy story into a serious drama.

- Don't forget what your readers like within your chosen genre.

Example: Ignoring the fact that fans of science fiction stories often enjoy futuristic settings and advanced technology.

THE STRUGGLES WITH WRITING IN A GENRE

Navigating expectations: It's challenging to balance meeting readers' expectations with introducing fresh elements that keep the story engaging.

Crafting unique characters: Creating characters that fit the genre while also being distinct and memorable can be a challenging task for writers.

YOUR TURN

Now pick the genre you would like to write your children's story in, and write a few sentences about why you chose this genre.

SETTING

SETTING

Where does your story take place?

The setting in a children's story is like the background of a painting — it helps create the mood and atmosphere of the story. It's where the characters live, play, and have their adventures.

A well-chosen setting can make the story more vivid and exciting, drawing young readers into the world of the story and making it feel real. It also helps children to better understand the characters and their actions, and it can teach them about different places and cultures.

So, the setting is an important part of any children's story, helping to make it memorable and engaging.

You can set your story in the past, present or future.

Making it timeless is a good way of avoiding alienating your reader. If you make it too specific readers may struggle to relate. Think of **'Charlie and the Chocolate Factory.'** It's timeless.

If you do set your story at a particular point in history, make sure you do your research – This makes it authentic.

You can set it in the mundane and normal – for example, in a hospital. But stick to your story and don't get caught up in sub-plots. **One story, one mission.**

Try to stick to 1-2 settings to give a sense of place – too many settings and your reader may get confused.

Think of setting your story in an adult setting but with a child's view. For example, a bank robbery, racing cars etc.

FAMOUS SETTINGS (AND WHY KIDS LIKE THEM!)

- **Hogwarts School of Witchcraft and Wizardry:** A magical castle where children learn spells and have exciting adventures, appealing to their imagination and love for magic.

- **Hundred Acre Wood:** A forest where Winnie-the-Pooh and friends explore, teaching children about friendship and the wonders of nature.

- **Narnia:** A magical world with talking animals and thrilling adventures, sparking children's curiosity and sense of wonder.

- **Neverland:** An island where children never grow up and go on adventures with pirates and fairies, igniting their sense of adventure and freedom.

- **The Land of Oz:** A colourful land with fantastical creatures and epic journeys, captivating children with its sense of discovery and imagination.

WHAT HAPPENS IF YOU DON'T THINK ABOUT YOUR SETTING?

Without considering the setting in a children's story, the world remains bland and undefined, lacking the magic and adventure that draws young readers in.

WHAT WE DID

For 'Katie and the Kite,' we already knew what kind of story it would be.

A kite is likely to be flown in a park. So we mentioned the park and her bedroom.

They were the only 2 settings.

KEY THINGS TO REMEMBER

- **Imagination ignition:** Settings should spark a child's imagination, transporting them to magical worlds or exciting adventures.

- **Mood and atmosphere:** Settings set the mood and atmosphere of the story, influencing how children feel and engage with the narrative.

- **Learning opportunity:** Settings can be a valuable tool for teaching children about different cultures, environments, and experiences, enriching their understanding of the world around them.

WHAT NOT TO DO

- Don't neglect to think about the setting, as it's crucial for creating a vivid and immersive world.

- Avoid using generic or uninspired settings that fail to spark a child's imagination.

- Don't forget to tailor the setting to fit the tone and theme of your story, as it enhances the overall experience for young readers.

- Avoid inconsistencies or unrealistic elements in the setting, which can disrupt the flow of the story and confuse young readers.

- Don't overlook the opportunity to use the setting to teach children about different cultures, environments, and experiences.

MOST COMMON SETTINGS

CHILDREN'S PICTURE BOOKS	Colourful and bustling city. Cosy countryside farm. Enchanting forest. Magical underwater world. Imaginative outer space adventure. Local park.
FANTASY	Enchanted forest with talking animals. Ancient and mysterious castle. Mythical kingdom with towering castles and bustling marketplaces. Hidden magical island with secret treasures. Otherworldly realm filled with floating islands and mystical creatures.
HUMOUR	Wacky and chaotic school. Silly and whimsical circus. Quirky and eccentric neighbourhood. Hilarious and unpredictable zoo. Outrageous and fantastical amusement park.
SPACE ADVENTURE	Futuristic space station with high-tech gadgets. Unexplored alien planet with strange landscapes. Interstellar spaceship travelling through the cosmos. Intergalactic city bustling with alien lifeforms. Cosmic adventure on a distant moon or asteroid.
FARM	A bustling farmyard with barns, pastures, and fields where animals roam freely and work together.

MOST COMMON SETTINGS

FAIRYTALES	Magical kingdom ruled by a benevolent king and queen. Enchanted cottage hidden deep in the woods. Towering castle guarded by a fearsome dragon. Mystical garden with talking animals and whimsical flora. Faraway land beyond the mountains with hidden treasures and ancient secrets.
MYSTERY	Creepy and atmospheric haunted mansion. Foggy and mysterious moorland. Bustling and chaotic city streets. Quiet and quaint village with hidden secrets. Spooky and eerie graveyard shrouded in mist.
ANIMAL STORIES	Lush and vibrant jungle teeming with life. Rolling hills and meadows of a countryside farm. Snow-covered Arctic landscape with polar bears and penguins. Exotic savannah with roaming lions and elephants. Dense and mysterious rainforest with colourful birds and playful monkeys.
FOREST	A lush and magical forest filled with towering trees, colourful flowers, and friendly woodland creatures.
CITY	Vibrant city streets bustling with activity, including shops, parks, and diverse communities.
UNDER THE SEA	An enchanting underwater world teeming with colourful coral reefs, exotic fish, and playful sea creatures.
HAUNTED HOUSE	A spooky old mansion filled with ghosts, ghouls, and other supernatural surprises waiting to be discovered.

MOST COMMON SETTINGS

JUNGLE	A dense jungle alive with exotic plants, winding rivers, and an array of wild animals swinging from the trees.
SPACE	The vast expanse of outer space, featuring planets, stars, and whimsical alien creatures on faraway worlds.
ENCHANTED CASTLE	A majestic castle surrounded by lush gardens, secret passages, and inhabited by royalty, knights, and magical beings.
ARCTIC/ ANTARCTIC	A frozen landscape of icy tundra, towering glaciers, and adorable polar animals like penguins, seals, and polar bears.
DESERT	The barren but beautiful desert landscape with rolling sand dunes, cacti, and intriguing desert creatures like camels and snakes.
FAIRYTALE VILLAGE	A charming village straight out of a fairytale, complete with cosy cottages, winding cobblestone streets, and mystical creatures.
OUTER SPACE	A futuristic world of spaceships, robots, and adventures among the stars.
ISLAND PARADISE	A tropical island paradise with palm trees, sandy beaches, and crystal-clear waters inhabited by friendly animals and colourful birds.
MAGICAL GARDEN	A whimsical garden filled with enchanted flowers, talking animals, and mystical creatures like fairies and gnomes.
PREHISTORIC LAND	A land lost in time where dinosaurs roam, featuring lush jungles, towering volcanoes, and thrilling adventures.

YOUR TURN

You have picked your genre, now pick your favourite idea of a setting within that genre and write a few sentences about why you chose this.

THEMES

THEMES

In children's stories, themes are the underlying messages or ideas that the story explores.

These themes can include concepts such as friendship, bravery, kindness, perseverance, and the importance of family.

Themes help children understand the deeper meaning of the story and may teach them valuable lessons or morals.

Themes must have:

- Clarity: Choose a clear and simple theme that children can easily understand and relate to.

- Relevance: Ensure the theme is relevant to children's lives, experiences, and developmental stages.

- Engagement: Integrate the theme organically into the storyline and characters to captivate and resonate with young readers.

FAMOUS EXAMPLES OF THEMES IN STORIES

Friendship:
- In 'Charlotte's Web,' the pig Wilbur forms an unlikely friendship with a spider named Charlotte. Charlotte helps Wilbur by weaving messages into her web, teaching children about loyalty and compassion.

Courage:
- In 'The Wizard of Oz,' Dorothy and her companions demonstrate bravery as they journey through the Land of Oz. Their adventures teach children about the power of courage and determination.

WHAT HAPPENS IF YOU DON'T INCLUDE A THEME?

If you don't include a theme in your children's story, it may lack depth and fail to resonate with young readers. Themes provide a central message or idea that children can connect with and learn from, making the story more meaningful and impactful.

Without a theme, the story may feel disjointed or aimless, missing the opportunity to teach valuable lessons or spark important conversations with children.

Additionally, themes help children relate the story to their own lives and experiences, fostering empathy, understanding, and emotional growth.

WHAT NOT TO DO

- Don't forget to have a theme. It helps make the story more interesting.
- Avoid putting a theme that doesn't really fit the story.
- Don't make the theme too hard for kids to understand.
- Avoid telling kids what the theme is too directly.

Example: In a story about friendship, don't suddenly switch to talking about bravery without any reason. It might confuse kids and make the story less enjoyable.

WHAT WE DID

When it came to our story, 'Katie and the Kite,' we wanted it to be about friendship, kindness and perseverance as we thought they were important lessons.

We then thought of a way we could SHOW those themes without directly telling.

In our story, Katie gave away the kite she found to a little girl.

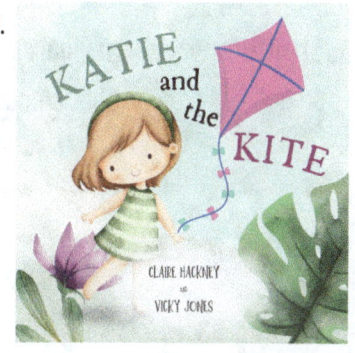

LIST OF COMMON THEMES

FRIENDSHIP	COURAGE	KINDNESS	IMAGINATION	PERSEVERANCE
ACCEPTANCE	FAMILY	BELONGING	ADVENTURE	DISCOVERY
GROWING UP	IDENTITY	EMPATHY	CO-OPERATION	HONESTY
PROBLEM-SOLVING	LOVE	FORGIVENESS	HOPE	INDEPENDENCE

THEME	STORY BOOK EXAMPLE
KINDNESS	'The Giving Tree' by Shel Silverstein – A tree selflessly gives everything to a boy she loves, showcasing themes of love and sacrifice.
IMAGINATION	'Where the Wild Things Are' by Maurice Sendak – Max imagines a world of wild creatures in his bedroom, leading to a magical adventure that celebrates the power of imagination.
PERSEVERANCE	'The Little Engine That Could' by Watty Piper – A small train engine overcomes obstacles and perseveres in her journey to deliver toys to children, teaching the value of determination and hard work.
ACCEPTANCE	'Wonder' by R.J. Palacio – Auggie Pullman, a boy with facial differences, navigates the challenges of fitting in at a new school, teaching children about acceptance and embracing differences.

LIST OF COMMON THEMES

THEME	STORY BOOK EXAMPLE
FAMILY	'The Family Book' by Todd Parr – Celebrates the diversity of families, teaching children that families come in all shapes, sizes, and forms.
BELONGING	'The Ugly Duckling' by Hans Christian Andersen – A duckling struggles to fit in with his family until he discovers he's actually a swan, teaching children about finding their place in the world.
ADVENTURE	'Alice's Adventures in Wonderland' by Lewis Carroll – Alice falls down a rabbit hole into a whimsical world filled with fantastical creatures and strange adventures, inspiring children to embrace curiosity and exploration.
DISCOVERY	'Oh, the Places You'll Go!' by Dr. Seuss – Encourages children to embrace new experiences and discover the world around them as they journey through life.
GROWING UP	'Peter Pan' by J.M. Barrie – Peter Pan and the Darling children learn about the joys and challenges of growing up, teaching children about the passage of time and the importance of cherishing childhood.
IDENTITY	'Giraffes Can't Dance' by Giles Andreae – Gerald the giraffe learns to embrace his uniqueness and discover his own rhythm, teaching children about self-acceptance and celebrating individuality.
EMPATHY	'The Invisible Boy' by Trudy Ludwig – Brian, an invisible boy, learns to find his voice and make friends with the help of a new student who reaches out to him, teaching children about empathy and inclusion.

LIST OF COMMON THEMES

THEME	STORY BOOK EXAMPLE
CO-OPERATION	'Swimmy' by Leo Lionni – Swimmy, a small fish, teaches his fellow fish to work together to outsmart a predator, showing children the importance of cooperation and teamwork.
HONESTY	'The Boy Who Cried Wolf' – A boy learns the consequences of lying when no one believes him after falsely claiming there's a wolf, teaching children the value of honesty and trustworthiness.
PROBLEM-SOLVING	'The Three Little Pigs' – Three pigs must use their creativity and resourcefulness to build houses that can withstand the huffing and puffing of the Big Bad Wolf, teaching children about problem-solving.
LOVE	'Guess How Much I Love You' by Sam McBratney – Little Nutbrown Hare and Big Nutbrown Hare express their love for each other in this heartwarming story about the depth of love between parent and child.
FORGIVENESS	'The Forgiveness Garden' by Lauren Thompson – Two friends learn to forgive each other after a falling out by tending to a garden together, teaching children about the healing power of forgiveness and reconciliation.
INDEPENDENCE	'The Runaway Bunny' by Margaret Wise Brown – A little bunny explores his independence while his mother lovingly reassures him that she will always be there for him, teaching children about the balance between independence and security.

MORE THEMES

KINDNESS	SHARING	COURAGE
BRAVERY	OVERCOMING FEARS	PERSEVERANCE
FRIENDSHIP	EMPATHY	HONESTY
RESPECT	GRATITUDE	GENEROSITY
COMPASSION	RESPONSIBILITY	PATIENCE
COOPERATION	DIVERSITY	CREATIVITY
IMAGINATION	FORGIVENESS	PROBLEM-SOLVING
LOVE	ADVENTURE	ACCEPTANCE
IDENTITY	ENVIRONMENTAL CONSERVATION	NATURE
TEAMWORK	GROWING UP	DREAMS AND ASPIRATIONS
DEALING WITH CHANGE	MAKING MISTAKES	LEARNING FROM MISTAKES
CELEBRATING ACHIEVEMENTS	SELF-ESTEEM	DEATH/LOSS

HOW TO USE THEMES

FRIENDSHIP	A story about two characters who help each other through challenges and have fun together, teaching the value of loyalty and support.
COURAGE	A character faces their fears to help a friend or overcome an obstacle, showing bravery and determination.
KINDNESS	A character performs small acts of kindness towards others, such as sharing toys or helping someone in need, demonstrating the importance of compassion and empathy.
IMAGINATION	A story about a child who uses their imagination to go on magical adventures or create fantastical worlds, inspiring creativity and wonder.
PERSEVERANCE	A character encounters obstacles but keeps trying until they succeed, teaching the value of determination and resilience.
ACCEPTANCE	A story where characters learn to accept and celebrate each other's differences, promoting inclusivity and understanding.
FAMILY	A tale about the love and support within a family, highlighting the bonds between parents and children or siblings.
BELONGING	A character feels out of place but discovers a group where they feel accepted and valued, emphasising the importance of finding one's place in the world.
ADVENTURE	A story about characters who embark on an exciting journey filled with discovery and excitement, encouraging curiosity and exploration.
DISCOVERY	Characters learn new things about themselves or the world around them, fostering a sense of curiosity and wonder.

HOW TO USE THEMES

GROWING UP	A character experiences changes and challenges as they navigate the journey from childhood to adulthood, exploring themes of maturity and responsibility.
IDENTITY	A story where characters embrace their unique qualities and learn to be true to themselves, promoting self-acceptance and confidence.
EMPATHY	Characters show understanding and compassion towards others, considering their feelings and perspectives.
COOPERATION	Characters work together to achieve a common goal, demonstrating teamwork and collaboration.
HONESTY	A character learns the importance of telling the truth, even when it's difficult, and faces the consequences of dishonesty.
PROBLEM-SOLVING	Characters encounter challenges and use their ingenuity and resourcefulness to find solutions, promoting critical thinking skills.
LOVE	A story about the deep bond between characters, whether it's between family members, friends, or even pets, emphasising the power of love and connection.
FORGIVENESS	Characters learn to forgive each other after conflicts or misunderstandings, promoting healing and reconciliation.
INDEPENDENCE	A character gains confidence and self-reliance as they learn to do things on their own, fostering a sense of autonomy and freedom.
HOPE	Characters face adversity but maintain optimism and resilience, inspiring readers to believe in brighter futures.

YOUR TURN

Look at the THEMES and storyline ideas and pick your favourite.

Then jot down some ideas of how you could SHOW these themes.

EMOTIONS

WHY ENCOURAGE EMOTIONS IN A CHILDREN'S STORY?

The purpose of emotions in children's stories is to engage young readers, evoke empathy, and help them navigate and understand their own feelings.

Emotions add depth and resonance to characters and situations, making the story more relatable and impactful.

Additionally, experiencing a range of emotions in stories can help children develop emotional intelligence and coping skills in life.

WHICH EMOTIONS COULD YOU USE IN YOUR STORY?

HAPPINESS	SADNESS	ANGER	FEAR	SURPRISE
DISGUST	EXCITEMENT	LOVE	ANXIETY	CURIOSITY

EMOTION	EXAMPLE
HAPPINESS	In 'Harry Potter and the Philosopher's Stone' by J.K. Rowling, Harry receives his acceptance letter to Hogwarts School of Witchcraft and Wizardry and feels overjoyed and excited about the magical world he's about to enter.
SADNESS	In 'Charlotte's Web' by E.B. White, Wilbur the pig feels deeply saddened when he learns that his friend Charlotte the spider has passed away, leaving behind her egg sac.
ANGER	In 'Where the Wild Things Are' by Maurice Sendak, Max feels angry when he's sent to his room without supper, prompting him to retreat to his imagination where he becomes king of the Wild Things.

EMOTIONS

EMOTION	EXAMPLE
FEAR	In 'The Lion, the Witch and the Wardrobe' by C.S. Lewis, Lucy feels fear when she first encounters the White Witch in the snowy forest of Narnia, uncertain of what danger lies ahead.
SURPRISE	In 'Alice's Adventures in Wonderland' by Lewis Carroll, Alice feels surprised when she shrinks down to a tiny size after drinking from a bottle labeled "Drink Me," leading to her adventures in Wonderland.
DISGUST	In 'Green Eggs and Ham' by Dr. Seuss, the unnamed character feels disgust at the thought of eating green eggs and ham, refusing to try them until the end of the story when he discovers he actually enjoys them.
EXCITEMENT	In 'The Polar Express' by Chris Van Allsburg, the children feel excited as they board the magical train bound for the North Pole, eager to meet Santa Claus and experience the wonders of Christmas.
LOVE	In 'Guess How Much I Love You' by Sam McBratney, Little Nutbrown Hare and Big Nutbrown Hare express their love for each other by trying to outdo one another with grand gestures, demonstrating the depth of their affection.
ANXIETY	In 'The Very Hungry Caterpillar' by Eric Carle, the caterpillar feels anxious as he spins himself into a cocoon, uncertain of what will happen next as he undergoes a transformation.
CURIOSITY	In 'Curious George' by H.A. Rey and Margret Rey, George the monkey feels curious as he explores the world around him, getting into mischief and learning new things along the way.

WHAT HAPPENS IF YOU DON'T INCLUDE EMOTIONS?

If you don't use emotions in children's stories, the narratives may feel flat and fail to connect with young readers on a deeper level.

Emotions play a crucial role in engaging children and helping them relate to the characters and situations in the story.

WHAT TO DO

- **Authenticity:** Ensure emotions are relatable and not exaggerated.
- **Balance:** Use both words and illustrations to convey emotions effectively.
- **Resolution:** Provide opportunities for emotions to be addressed and resolved within the story.

WHAT NOT TO DO

- Don't ignore or downplay the importance of emotions in storytelling, as they are essential for engaging young readers.
- Avoid using overly complex or intense emotions that may overwhelm or confuse children.
- Don't rely solely on external events to convey emotions; ensure characters' internal thoughts and feelings are also explored.
- Don't shy away from addressing difficult emotions, but ensure they are handled in a sensitive and age-appropriate manner.

WHAT CAN CAUSE EMOTIONS IN STORIES?

EMOTION	EXAMPLE
HAPPINESS	Finding a lost puppy, receiving a surprise gift, or spending time with friends and family.
SADNESS	Losing a beloved toy, saying goodbye to a friend who is moving away, or feeling left out of a group activity.
ANGER	Being teased or bullied by others, having something taken away unfairly, or feeling frustrated when things don't go as planned.
FEAR	Encountering a scary animal, hearing strange noises at night, or being in a dark and unfamiliar place.
SURPRISE	Discovering a hidden treasure, meeting a new friend unexpectedly, or receiving a surprise visit from a relative.
DISGUST	Coming across something slimy or gross, tasting a food that they don't like, or encountering a foul smell.
EXCITEMENT	Going on a thrilling adventure, attending a fun event like a carnival or amusement park, or anticipating a special occasion like a birthday party.
LOVE	Receiving hugs and kisses from family members, cuddling with a pet, or sharing a special moment with a best friend.
ANXIETY	Starting a new school or activity, facing a test or performance, or being separated from a caregiver in a crowded place.
CURIOSITY	Discovering a mysterious object, hearing a strange noise coming from the attic, or wondering what's inside a locked box.

HOW TO SHOW DIFFERENT EMOTIONS IN STORIES?

EMOTION	HOW TO SHOW IT
HAPPINESS	Smiling, laughing, jumping up and down, clapping their hands, or expressing excitement with wide eyes and a big grin.
SADNESS	Frowning, crying, sniffing, slumping shoulders, looking downcast, or seeking comfort from a caregiver.
ANGER	Frowning, clenching fists, stomping feet, yelling, throwing objects, or expressing frustration through tense body language.
FEAR	Trembling, shaking, wide-eyed, freezing in place, seeking comfort from a caregiver, or trying to hide or avoid the source of fear.
SURPRISE	Gasping, eyes widening, mouth dropping open, jumping back, or expressing disbelief with raised eyebrows and a shocked expression.
DISGUST	Grimacing, wrinkling nose, sticking out tongue, recoiling, or covering their mouth or nose to avoid an unpleasant smell or sight.
EXCITEMENT	Bouncing up and down, clapping hands, talking quickly, giggling, wide eyes, or a big smile with lots of energy.
LOVE	Hugging tightly, cuddling, kissing, holding hands, smiling warmly, or expressing affectionate words like "I love you."
ANXIETY	Biting nails, fidgeting, pacing back and forth, avoiding eye contact, trembling, or seeking reassurance from a caregiver.
CURIOSITY	Wide-eyed, leaning in closely, asking lots of questions, exploring with hands or eyes, or focusing intently on something new or interesting.

YOUR TURN

Look at the EMOTIONS section in your resources at the back of this workbook.

Pick a couple of your favourites and jot down some ideas of how you could SHOW these emotions in your writing.

OTHER WAYS TO GENERATE IDEAS

OTHER WAYS TO GENERATE IDEAS

Ideas are EVERYWHERE!

But sometimes we have a 'creativity block.'

Adults may struggle with generating fresh and imaginative story ideas that resonate with children, often due to being disconnected from the child's perspective or finding it challenging to think outside conventional narrative structures.

THINK: Does your idea actually excite you enough to write it, let alone for the reader to read it?

There are many ways to generate fresh and exciting ideas.

Ideas can be from anywhere and everywhere.

You don't HAVE to be creative to get story ideas.

Just observe your surroundings.

You have to seek ideas – be active.

An easy way to generate an idea is simply to add 'What if?' in front of anything.

And then...

OTHER WAYS TO GENERATE IDEAS

- **Embrace creativity:** Let your imagination run wild and explore fantastical ideas.

- **Tap into childhood:** Draw inspiration from the experiences, emotions, and fantasies of childhood.

- **Keep it simple:** Focus on straightforward plots and relatable themes that children can understand.

- **Add humour:** Infuse your story with humour and whimsy to engage young readers and listeners.

- **Include a moral:** Incorporate valuable lessons or morals that resonate with children and teach important life lessons.

- **Use rhyme and rhythm:** Experiment with rhyme and rhythm to create catchy phrases and memorable storytelling.

- **Incorporate diversity:** Reflect diverse characters and perspectives to promote inclusivity and representation.

- **Stay curious:** Be open to new ideas and perspectives, and always be curious about the world around you.

- **Test your ideas:** Share your story ideas with children or childlike adults to gauge their interest and feedback.

- **Have fun:** Enjoy the process of storytelling and let your passion for creativity shine through in your work.

OTHER WAYS TO GENERATE IDEAS

Start from the 'normal'.

You get a visitor at your door:

- Who is it at the door?
- What if something was different?
- What if they had brought a magical gift?
- They had a dog with them; what if the pet could talk and then tells people where magical secret passageways are...?

The mundane can be transformed into something exciting.

In fact, the more mundane, the more fun it is to be something magical!

Start with 'boring' things such as 'socks.'

We once had the idea for a children's story about a magical place where all the lost socks go! (We were going to call it 'The Land of the Lost Socks').

Think of adventure in the most unlikely of places –

Narnia in the wardrobe, for example.

or:

What if the shed in the garden had something magical inside..?

And then it went missing?

OTHER WAYS TO GENERATE IDEAS

IDEAS TO GET YOU THINKING

TREEHOUSE	High above the ground, a group of animal friends build a treehouse where they gather to share stories and go on exciting adventures. When a storm threatens to destroy their beloved treehouse, they must work together to save it.
ATTIC	While exploring their grandparents' attic, two siblings stumble upon a dusty old chest filled with magical artefacts. As they uncover the history behind each object, they unlock the key to restoring magic to their family's lineage
PARK BENCH	Every day, an elderly man sits on a park bench feeding pigeons and sharing stories with the children who pass by. Through his tales, the children learn valuable lessons about kindness, empathy, and the importance of cherishing memories.
BASEMENT	A group of neighbourhood kids discover a hidden door in the basement of an old mansion, leading to a mysterious underground world filled with fantastical creatures. Together, they must navigate through challenges and obstacles to find their way back home.
BACKYARD SHED	When a mischievous squirrel steals a magical acorn from a backyard shed, it unwittingly unleashes chaos upon the neighbourhood. With the help of their animal friends, a group of children embark on a quest to retrieve the acorn and restore peace to their backyard.
LIBRARY CORNER	A book-loving mouse living in a library discovers a hidden tunnel behind the shelves that leads to a world where books come to life. As they journey through different literary landscapes, they learn valuable lessons about courage, friendship, and the power of storytelling.
TOY BOX	In a toy box filled with forgotten toys, a brave teddy bear leads a group of playthings on a quest to find their missing owner. Along the way, they encounter obstacles and challenges that test their loyalty and friendship.
KITCHEN CUPBOARD	When a curious cat sneaks into the kitchen cupboard, it accidentally spills a potion that brings kitchen utensils to life. Chaos ensues as the utensils embark on a hilarious adventure through the kitchen, learning valuable lessons about teamwork and cooperation.

OTHER WAYS TO GENERATE IDEAS

Think of what children are doing at that age – waving, clapping, pointing.

- Who or what are they waving at?
- Is it only them who can see something?
- What made them clap with delight?
- What are they pointing at?
- Are they excited or scared?

Try to include this in your story idea.

Explore your local area, people watch, and then say 'imagine if...' or 'what would happen if...' to everything! Something will stick.

What if that boy on the skateboard suddenly took off into the air and then went to outer space for a while..?

DIFFERENCES AND OPPOSITES

Combine seemingly different ideas together and see what you come up with.

Like cooking with 2 strange ingredients.

Like worms and gravy (yuk!)

Does it make a special potion with powers?

CHARACTERS

Start with a character - we did for 'Katie and the Kite.'

Ask questions about them.

- What is something unique or interesting about them?
- What secret do they have?
- What happens if that secret gets out?

OR:

- Did somebody you know wear a funny hat?
- Funny waistcoat?
- What did they always do?

OR:

If you see a dog, ask questions about the owner.

- Are they a lorry driver?
- A burglar?
- What if they got their dog to help them with stealing things?

Think of your character - then think of what problem they have and what they need to do to solve it - this creates a very basic plot!

MY CHARACTER NEEDS TO..

BUT WHAT IF...? ....

AND THEN? ....

CHARACTERS

My character (an alien) needs to get back to Mars.

But what if the spaceship was damaged?

And then a little boy saw the alien, got scared at first then helped him get back to Mars.

SETTINGS

Start with a setting.

Fields, farms, schools, etc.

What happens at night?

What if instead of humans going to school, animals did?

What if animals made different noises?

ANIMALS

Think of animals that NEED each other to achieve a mission.

Eg: a mouse needs a cat to quickly take them to places to achieve a mission.

What could that mission be?

Mix and match.

This is especially interesting with animals who shouldn't like each other.

YOUR CHILDHOOD

Look at your own childhood.

Was there a strange cupboard under the stairs?

What 'could' be in there that would make an interesting story?

Was there a strange man/woman in your street?

YOUR FEARS

What were your irrational fears when you were young?

A person, a noise, the swimming pool?

Did you used to think there was a SHARK in the swimming pool?

- Was it the cupboard under the stairs that scared you?
- Was it the shed?
- Was it a spooky cat?

List them and think of a story around that idea. Ask: What if... there was a bear in the shed?

And then he came out of the shed looking for food...?

When you were 5, 6, 10 or 11 years old, what did you care about?

- What did you get sad about? What if...? And then...?
- What were you curious about? What if...? And then...?
- What scared you? What if...? And then...?
- What stories did you make up? What if...? And then...?
- What fears did you have? What if...? And then...?

OLD PHOTOGRAPHS

Look at old photographs, and think about the locations. What if...? And then...?

What were you thinking at the time? What if...? And then...?

Turn some stories on their head. What if...? And then...?

What if INSTEAD of this happening, THIS happened...

And then...

RELATIONSHIPS

Think of your relationships when you were young.

Your pets, your favourite toy, a school teacher who was kind or who was strange.

Now think of a story based around those ideas.

Start with 'What if?.... and 'and then...?'

SMELLS

Think of the smells of your childhood - baking, vegetables, fields, flowers etc.

What settings make you think of these?

What could start a story?

WELL-KNOWN STORIES

Use stories you like and flip them to change them into a completely different story - different ending, different villain etc.

Rewrite old stories - BUT DO NOT COPY THEM.

This will land you in trouble. Use them for inspiration only.

MOVIES

Think of stories/films you like today - even horror stories - and then water the storylines down to where you could use them as inspiration in a children's story.

Think of the locations of those stories - a hotel, a ship etc. What if...? And then...?

Write a couple of lines to describe the original and then write, "Instead of them doing... They do this instead..."

THE NEWS

Look at the news - national and local. Can you flip the story and make it something funny or unusual?

Always think: 'What if...?'

News story = **Farmers planting trees to create more woodlands**

What if a group of farmers discovered magical seeds that turned their fields into a vibrant woodland, where the animals can speak? And then, the seeds get stolen...

Lone sailor 20 miles off Cornish coast rescued

What if a young boy, aged 7, found himself adrift at sea, 20 miles off the Cornish coast until a brave rescue brought him back to safety? Along his perilous journey, he encounters magical creatures of the sea - talking dolphins, wise turtles, etc. who guide him through the waves and teach him the importance of kindness.

Through his encounters with these enchanting beings, the boy discovers a newfound appreciation for the wonders of the sea and wants to help sea creatures. (Theme - environmental).

PEOPLE WATCHING

Ask questions about them.

What if they were actually a... GHOST.

Where are they going? TO PLAY TRICKS ON PEOPLE.

What if they had a secret? THEY KNEW WHERE ALL THE MISSING PEOPLE IN THE WORLD WERE.

What if they had a superpower? WITH A BLINK, EVERYONE WOULD BE IN FUNNY CLOTHES!

OPPOSITES

The idea of a Granny being a big-time burglar.

A mouse scaring off lions etc...

Think of opposites and how they can work.

EXAMPLES OF OPPOSITES

A gentle giant who is afraid of tiny insects.	A fearless kitten who befriends a group of intimidating wolves.
A clumsy acrobat who becomes the star of the circus.	A shy dragon who prefers gardening over breathing fire.
A wise owl who is afraid of the dark.	A tiny ant who outwits a cunning fox.
A grumpy fairy who spreads joy wherever she goes.	A timid lion who leads the other animals in daring adventures.
A strict teacher who loves playing pranks on the students.	A mischievous ghost who is terrified of humans.

"I'M NOT ALLOWED IT... SO I WANT IT"

Children are drawn to the things they are not supposed to have -

- Their toys at bedtime.

- Sweets before dinner.

- Fast cars etc.

- Too much TV.

What does your child, grandchild, niece/nephew, or friend's child always want?

THINGS THAT CHILDREN WANT, BUT AT TIMES THEY MAY NOT BE ABLE TO HAVE

Sugary treats.	Staying up late past bedtime.
Playing with potentially dangerous items or objects.	Watching TV shows or movies that are deemed inappropriate.
Going to exciting places without parental supervision.	Playing with messy substances like paints or mud indoors.
Using sharp or breakable items without supervision.	Having pets that requires a lot of care and responsibility.
Eating fast food or unhealthy snacks frequently.	Using electronic devices for extended periods of time.

What if your character wanted sugary treats?

What if your character found a never-ending sweet jar by going on an adventure?

They encounter lots of different characters along the way. They eventually get to the sweet jar.

And then they eat too much and get a tummy ache.

Moral: Moderation and healthy eating.

"I'M NOT ALLOWED IT... SO I WANT IT"

What if your character wanted to stay up late past bedtime?

What if your character found a special flashlight to stay up at night?

And then they are too tired the next day for something fun and fall asleep.

<u>Moral/theme</u>: Importance of sleep for health.

What if your character wanted to go to exciting places without parental supervision?

And then your character found a treasure map?

They get lost or encounter danger.

<u>Theme</u>: Safety and staying together.

FOOD

Food can be an interesting idea.

What if your character's favourite pizza place ran out of pizza?

And then they must find a way to make their own pizza from scratch, using weird food.

<u>Moral/theme</u>: Learning to be resourceful and independent in solving problems.

What if your character's chicken nuggets were stolen by a mischievous bird?

And then they have to come up with a plan to retrieve their chicken nuggets and go on an adventure.

<u>Moral/theme</u>: Understanding the importance of problem-solving and perseverance.

What if your character's chocolate chip cookies disappeared from the cookie jar?

And then they have to investigate who took the cookies and learn to share with others.

<u>Moral/theme</u>: Understanding the importance of honesty and sharing with others.

MIND MAP IDEAS

Start with a character, place, trait etc.

See where it takes you, circle some words, make up a story!

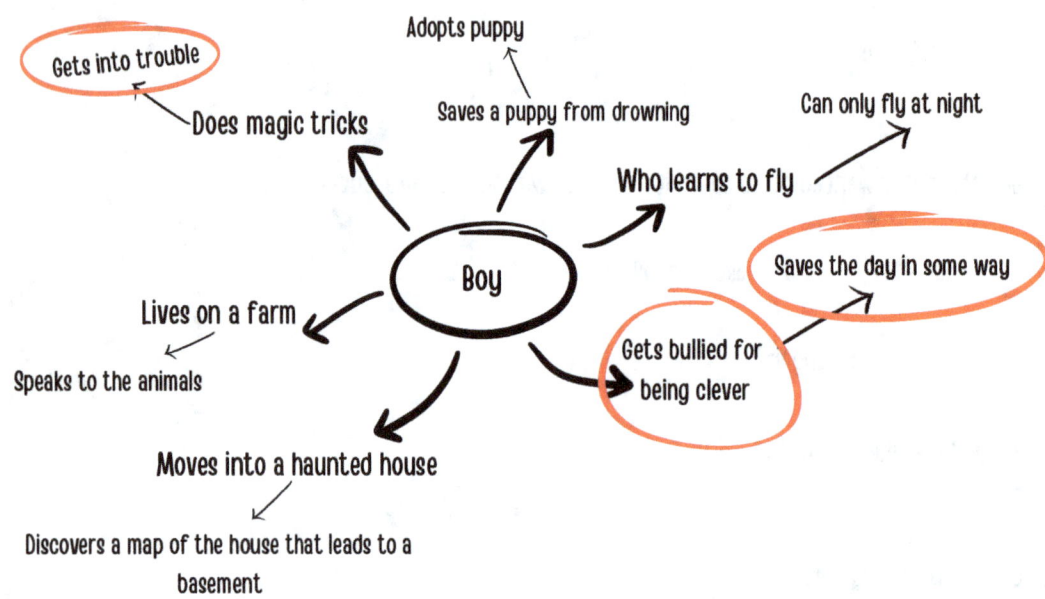

Words I have circled:

- Boy
- Bullied for being clever
- Gets into trouble
- Saves the day in some way

Let's start with 'What if...'

What if there was a boy, bullied for being clever who then thought it was better to just get into trouble like the bullies? And then, he found a hidden book in the library when in detention. The book was old and was on code-breaking. Suddenly, the school came under siege by a mysterious ghost that scared everybody, even the bullies, but using his knowledge and code-breaking skills, the boy saved the day and the ghost returned to where it belonged after the boy shouted out the spell from the code-breaking book.

Theme: Be yourself, don't change for anybody.

MORE IDEAS FOR YOUR MIND MAP

OVERCOMING A MONSTER	RAGS TO RICHES	A QUEST/MISSION	A VOYAGE AND RETURN
COMEDY	TRAGEDY	REBIRTH	COMING BACK FROM DANGER

CREATING IDEAS FROM OCCUPATIONS

DOCTOR	TEACHER	FIREFIGHTER	POLICE OFFICER	NURSE
CHEF	CONSTRUCTION	FARMER	ASTRONAUT	PILOT

What if an astronaut gets lost in space and then finds a magical planet?

An astronaut accidentally veers off course and discovers a new planet filled with talking magical creatures.

But the astronaut must find a way back home while navigating the wonders and dangers of the enchanted planet getting help from his new friends.

What if a farmer grows vegetables and then they start talking?

A farmer's vegetables come to life and start causing mischief on the farm.

Conflict arises when the farmer must figure out how to control their chatty crops and prevent them from taking over.

What if a teacher forgets everything they've ever learned and then the pupils start doing the teaching?

A teacher wakes up one day to find they've forgotten all their lessons and knowledge.

Conflict arises as they try to teach their class without any memory of how to do so, leading to humorous misunderstandings and creative teaching methods.

A CHILD'S DAY

Think of child's day –

- Getting up
- Bedtime
- Bath time
- Meal times
- Getting dressed
- Potty training
- Visitors

Write ideas around these times. Start with 'What if...?' and 'and then...?'

BATHTIME

What if bath time was a splashy safari adventure?

Each bath time, a child's bathtub transforms into a jungle river filled with toy animals.

And then the child must rescue their toy giraffe from the clutches of a mischievous rubber duck.

Moral: Bath time can be a wild and imaginative experience. Problem-solving.

LANGUAGE

Try writing the first words that come into your head that sound fun or rhyme:

boat, goat, crunch, scrunch, click, quick, whack, quack.

Think of 'The Goat in the Boat', and think of a journey: 'What if the goat had to get across the river?"

SOME WORDS TO GET YOU STARTED

MOON	ARROW	CLOCK
SPOON	SPARROW	ROCK
BALLOON	CARROT	LOCK
CARTOON	PARROT	PIG
ROOM	DUCK	WIG
BROOM	PUCK	FIG
GLOOM	TRUCK	DIG
MUSHROOM	STUCK	TWIG
BOOK	FROG	STAR
LOOK	LOG	CAR
COOK	DOG	JAR
HOOK	SOCK	BAR

The clock in the sock　　　The pig in the wig　　　The star in the jar

What if a pig on a farm stole the horrible farmer's wig, and locked the farmer in his pig pen? The pig, disguised as the farmer went to the shops and bought lots of nice food for him and the other animals.

And then, the shopkeeper started to notice something strange and followed the pig back to the farm where all the other animals played along and convinced the shopkeeper to leave. The farmer felt bad for how he treated the animals and they let him out and the farmer treated them better.

Mix and match. See which ones seem funny, and interesting.
Add a 'What if...?' and 'and then...?'

MORE IDEAS FOR STORIES

BROOM ➕ MOON

THE BROOM ON THE MOON

What if a witch left her broomstick on the moon **and then** asked a boy for help?

PIG ➕ WIG

THE PIG IN THE WIG

What if a pig found a wig and fooled everybody **and then** pretended they were a farmer to get more food for everybody?

SOME WORDS TO GET YOU STARTED

MAGICAL	CURIOUS	WACKY
ENCHANTING	SILLY	SWIRLY
MYSTERIOUS	GLOWING	SNAZZY
GIGANTIC	WONDROUS	ODDBALL
SPARKLING	AMAZING	COSMIC
DAZZLING	FRIENDLY	JAZZY
WHIMSICAL	ZANY	PERCULIA
FANTASTIC	BUBBLY	BIZARRE
SPECTACULAR	GROOVY	OUTLANDISH
COLOURFUL	QUIRKY	ECCENTRIC
BRAVE	FUNKY	BOISTEROUS
PLAYFUL	SPOOKY	LIVELY

Use these words to come up with idea like:

The Lively Lion's Safari
Wacky Warthog's Wild Adventure

The Peculiar Pelicans
The Jazzy Jellyfish

Oscar The Oddball Ostrich
The Groovy Gorilla

YOUR TURN

Pick 3-5 ideas and experiment. Create a mission or adventure with 'what if...?' and 'and then...?'

YOUR CHARACTERS

HUMANS, ANIMALS AND OBJECTS

YOUR CHARACTERS

A character in a children's story is a person, animal, or creature who plays a role in the plot.

They have unique traits, feelings, and actions that help move the story forward and make it interesting for young readers.

FAMOUS CHARACTERS IN CHILDREN'S STORIES

- Harry Potter: A young wizard at Hogwarts, who battles against the dark wizard Voldemort.

- Winnie the Pooh: A lovable bear who lives in the Hundred Acre Wood with friends like Piglet and Tigger.

- Alice: A curious girl who falls into a whimsical world in "Alice's Adventures in Wonderland."

CHARACTERS WHO AREN'T EVEN REAL/HUMAN

- The Little Engine That Could: A determined blue train.

- The Velveteen Rabbit: A stuffed rabbit who wants to be real.

- The Giving Tree: A generous tree.

- Ferdinand the Bull: A gentle bull who loves flowers.

WHAT HAPPENS IF YOU DON'T HAVE AN INTERESTING MAIN CHARACTER?

If the main character in a children's story isn't interesting, it can make the story less engaging.

Kids might lose interest and not connect with the plot or themes.

A dull main character can make it hard to keep the reader's attention, reducing the story's impact and success.

YOUR CHARACTERS

WHAT NOT TO DO WHEN IT COMES TO CREATING CHARACTERS

- Stereotypes: Avoid relying on clichés and narrow representations.

- Complexity overload: Keep characters relatable without overwhelming complexity.

- Stagnant characters: Ensure characters grow and evolve throughout the story. Always have a character arc.

- Inappropriate content: Stay mindful of age-appropriate themes and language.

- Lack of diversity: Embrace and celebrate diversity in characters' backgrounds and experiences

WHAT TO DO

The main thing for your main character is for them to have a goal.

What do they want/need to achieve in the story and why?

There has to be a point A to a point B.

CHARACTERS IN A STORY

- Protagonist = Main character.

- Villain = The baddie.

- Ally = The goodie/helper.

YOUR CHARACTERS

HOW TO CREATE INTERESTING STORIES USING CHARACTERS: FLIP THE SCRIPT

Turn the norm on its head - instead of a cat running from a dog, turn it around.

What if the dog always ran from the scary-looking cat and then one day, he faced his fear and stood up to the cat who said he only chased the dog because he thought he wanted to play?

THINGS TO REMEMBER WHEN CREATING INTERESTING CHARACTERS

- Keep characters approximately the same age as your target audience so they can identify with them.

- Stick to one or two main characters (three at most) so the story doesn't get confusing to a younger reader. You could start with a main character and a problem to overcome.

- Have a 'question' for your story.
    - Will my main character achieve their mission? Yes, by using all the resources available (list them) they will achieve their mission.
    - What is your story's question and answer? This can help with goals, obstacles and consequences.

YOUR CHARACTERS

YOUR VILLAIN

Your villain doesn't need to be a human. It doesn't even need to be a real living and breathing thing.

A villain is ANYTHING that is in the way of your main character achieving their goal.

A villain in a children's story is a character or element that opposes the protagonist (main character) creating conflict and obstacles to overcome.

Human villains are characters with malicious intentions, such as wicked witches or evil sorcerers.

Non-human villains can include elements like treacherous mountains, raging storms, or enchanted forests that thwart the protagonist's journey.

When you think of your villain - why are they bad?

- What is their goal?
- What is their specific bad behaviour?
- How could they be stopped?

You don't always need a villain. In a story you really just need a problem to overcome - this CAN be your villain but it doesn't have to be.

VILLAINS ARE GREAT FUN, BUT HOW BAD SHOULD THEY BE?

It is recommended that the villain gets justice in your story.

DOES YOUR VILLAIN REFORM AND BECOME A GOODIE?

They can do but don't make it too predictable and cheesy.

Villains are important. They power your story. The characters react to the villain and vice versa.

What is your villain's aim/goal? (if it is a character - think of Cruella de Vil, who wants to make puppies into fur coats).

YOUR CHARACTERS

YOUR VILLAIN

You can make your villains scary.

Make them gross! You want a reaction from your young reader.

What can the children see in a villain that the parents can't?

Some children's authors use a thesaurus to come up with names for their villains.

Think of the name 'Miss Trunchbull' in Matilda = Truncheon and Bull.

To come up with your own villain's name, try experimenting with their character traits, but don't make it obvious, make it unique.

Don't make your villain 100% bad all the time.

We use the 80/20 principle – 80% bad and 20% good. This makes them more human.

If you're thinking of writing a book series, then think about NOT killing off your villain.

YOUR CHARACTERS

YOUR ALLY

An ally in a children's story is a character or element that supports and aids the protagonist in achieving their goals.

Human allies can be friends, parents, teachers or mentors.

Non-human allies can include helpful animals, enchanted objects, or friendly spirits that assist the protagonist on their journey.

CHARACTERS IN KIDS BOOKS AREN'T AS IN-DEPTH AS THEY ARE IN NOVELS.

You simply don't have the word count to describe them.

Most can be summed up in 2 adjectives: funny and smart etc.

Your main character should be somebody your reader can identify with. Your main character is often a child, but not necessarily a human child. They can be a puppy, lion cub etc.

Think of your character's objective - keep them on a simple mission, don't overcomplicate - 'Katie and the Kite' was simply about Katie fixing a kite so that it would fly.

YOUR CHARACTERS

GOALS

Are you going to send your character somewhere? On a journey or quest?

- What is the destination?

- What could happen along the way? - the obstacles etc).

Your character's goal can be a simple journey.

You can sometimes end up back to the same place, but a change has occurred - physically, mentally, emotionally.

THE CIRCULAR PLOT

A journey doesn't have to be physical, it can be about growing up and discovering yourself.

Your main character may feel initially feel lost and then found (but in the same place). Think:

- Do they need something?
- Do they want something?
- Do they need healing from something?
- Do they need friends?
- Have they been (or get) bullied?
- Are they poor?

Take your character out of their comfort zone, and test them whether it's physically or mentally. If they are scared of a spooky cupboard, they HAVE to go in it for some reason.

- Does your character run away?
- Why do they run away?
- Who do they meet along the way?
- How and why do they change?
- What obstacles do they face along the way?

YOUR CHARACTERS

ANIMALS/OBJECTS

Animals are often used in children's book as the main character.

They often exhibit human characteristics.

You can give animals more independence than a child in a story.

Your character could be something strange eg: a drain monster, a potato, a pencil, a shoe etc.

Animals and objects are just children in disguise.

Make your character relatable but just a little bit strange:

- Maybe they can DISAPPEAR?

- Maybe they discover they can FREEZE PEOPLE?

- In certain situations, maybe your ANIMALS CAN TALK?

PARENTS

Try to free up the child to have an adventure without the parents/carers.

Otherwise, this can become restricting. Can you get rid of parents so the kids can have an adventure?

Maybe have the main character run away or discover a secret place?

YOUR TURN

Think of your main character. Now give your main character a main goal and some key traits.

Also, consider your villain and repeat the process.

Here is an example to get you started:

MAIN CHARACTER IS A	PUPPY
MAIN GOAL	HE WANTS TO GO TO THE MAGIC FARM
BECAUSE	HE HEARD IT HAS NEVER-ENDING TREATS AND STICKS
BUT THE	BIGGER DOG (VILLAIN) WANTS TO FOLLOW HIM AND EAT ALL THE TREATS HIMSELF
2 CHARACTER TRAITS	KIND AND CLUMSY

MY VILLAIN IS A	BIGGER DOG
MAIN GOAL	HE WANTS TO GO TO THE MAGIC FARM TOO AND WANTS TO FOLLOW THE MAIN CHARACTER AND EAT ALL THE TREATS HIMSELF
BECAUSE	HE IS HUNGRY
BUT THE	MAIN CHARACTER MEETS FRIENDS ALONG THE WAY WHO HELP HIM
2 CHARACTER TRAITS	STRONG AND SELFISH

YOUR TURN

Think of your main character. Now give your main character a main goal and some key traits.

Also, consider your villain and repeat the process.

MAIN CHARACTER IS A	
MAIN GOAL	
BECAUSE	
BUT THE	
2 CHARACTER TRAITS	

MY VILLAIN IS A	
MAIN GOAL	
BECAUSE	
BUT THE	
2 CHARACTER TRAITS	

YOUR TURN

Now write a basic character profile for your main character and villain so you know them really well. How old are they? What clothes do they wear? What traits do they have? Think about their fears, goals etc.

MAIN CHARACTER

My main character **is called:** ....

They are aged: ....

People describe her/him/them as: ....

He/she/they like to do (good/bad things): ....

He doesn't/she doesn't/they don't like: ....

Description of the clothes they wear: ....

Their main fears are: ....

Their main goal is: ....

VILLAIN

My villain **is called:** ....

They are aged: ....

People describe her/him/them as: ....

He/she/they like to do (good/bad things): ....

He doesn't/she doesn't/they don't like: ....

Description of the clothes they wear: ....

Their main fears are: ....

Their main goal is: ....

TITLES

TITLES

A title for a children's story is a brief, catchy phrase or sentence that serves as the name of the story.

It should be engaging, appealing, and reflective of the story's theme, characters, or central message, aiming to capture the attention and curiosity of young readers.

FAMOUS TITLES - AND WHY THEY ARE INTRIGUING

'The Secret Garden' by Frances Hodgson Burnett - The title hints at mystery and adventure, enticing kids with the idea of discovering hidden wonders.

'Alice's Adventures in Wonderland' by Lewis Carroll - The title promises an exciting journey into a fantastical world, sparking kids' imaginations and curiosity.

'Charlie and the Chocolate Factory' by Roald Dahl - The title is deliciously enticing, evoking images of sweets and treats, which immediately captures the attention and excitement of children.

WHAT HAPPENS IF YOUR TITLE ISN'T ENGAGING?

A bland title can result in your children's story being overlooked.

It might fail to spark interest, leading to fewer readers and less engagement.

In a crowded market, a captivating title is essential for grabbing attention and ensuring your story stands out.

WHAT TO DO

- Come up with a striking title. One that rolls easily off the tongue, like: 'Katie and the Kite.'

- Simple titles work best, with fewer words, and more clarity.

- Try to include the character and the mission, or the trait, and create a picture with your title. Think in opposites like 'Gangsta Granny' by David Walliams.

- Where possible, use alliteration, such as 'Charlie and the Chocolate Factory' which features the 'Ch' sound, and 'Awful Auntie' which features the 'Au' sound.

- 'Stop! Elephant! Stop!' is a better title than 'The Elephant Who Jumps In The Water.'

- Don't give away the story or punchline in the title.

- To make your title better, ask questions of your reader.

WHAT NOT TO DO

- Avoid vagueness or lack of inspiration in your title.

- Steer clear of titles that lack creativity or fail to reflect your story's essence.

- Avoid overly complex or difficult-to-pronounce titles.

- Refrain from titles that give away too much of the plot, spoiling the sense of discovery for readers.

HOW TO COME UP WITH A GREAT TITLE

- **Brainstorm keywords:** Generate a list of keywords or phrases related to your story's themes, characters, setting, or plot events. Think about words that evoke emotions or intrigue.

- **Use imagery and creativity:** Incorporate vivid imagery, playful language, or creative wordplay to make your title memorable and engaging. Think about how you can paint a picture in the reader's mind.

- **Consider audience appeal:** Keep your target audience in mind. What kind of title would attract children's attention and curiosity? Aim for something age-appropriate and relatable.

HOW WE DID IT

For 'Katie and the Kite' it was quite simple. We used alliteration.

The words in the title flow off the tongue easily.

It's almost as if the kite is a character and has its own personality.

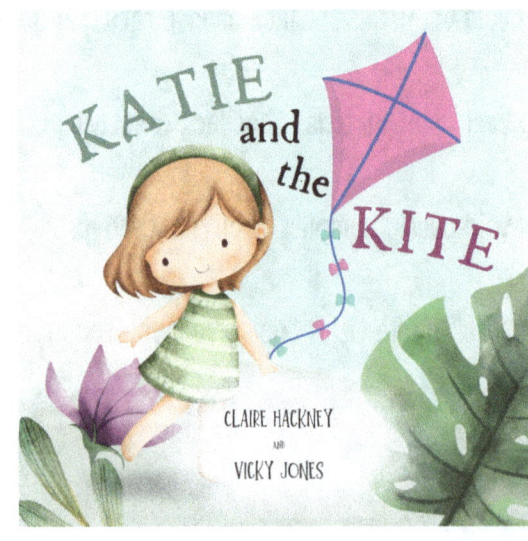

HOW TO COME UP WITH A GREAT TITLE

Creating engaging titles for children's picture books involves capturing the essence of the story while also piquing the curiosity and interest of potential readers.

Here are some tips to help you craft compelling titles:

REFLECT THE THEME OR MESSAGE	Consider the central theme or message of your picture book and try to convey it in the title. Choose words or phrases that reflect the heart of the story and give readers a glimpse of what to expect. For example, if your book is about friendship, a title like 'Adventures of the Best Friends' could be engaging.
USE DESCRIPTIVE LANGUAGE	Use descriptive language to evoke imagery and spark the imagination of readers. Think about the key elements of your story, such as characters, settings, or plot points, and incorporate them into the title. For example, if your book features a magical journey through the forest, a title like 'The Enchanted Woods Expedition' could be captivating.
CONSIDER ALLITERATION OR RHYME	Alliteration and rhyme can make titles more memorable and appealing to young readers. Play around with words that start with the same letter or have similar sounds to create catchy titles. For example, 'Silly Sally's Seaside Surprise,' or 'The Playful Penguin Parade' are both engaging titles that use alliteration.

HOW TO COME UP WITH A GREAT TITLE

CREATE A SENSE OF MYSTERY OR INTRIGUE

Intrigue readers by creating a sense of mystery or curiosity with your title.

Pose questions or hint at something unexpected to entice readers to want to learn more.

For example, 'The Secret Treasure of Dragon Island,' or 'Who Hid the Magic Key?' are titles that invite readers to uncover hidden mysteries within the story.

APPEAL TO EMOTIONS

Titles that evoke emotions or feelings can resonate with readers and draw them into the story.

Consider how your book makes readers feel and choose words that capture those emotions.

For example, 'The Little Lost Kitten's Quest for Home' appeals to readers' empathy and curiosity about the kitten's journey.

KEEP IT SHORT AND SWEET

Aim for titles that are concise and easy to remember, especially for young readers.

Avoid overly long or complicated titles that may be difficult for children to remember or pronounce.

Short and snappy titles are more likely to grab attention and stick in readers' minds.

A FORMULA TO HELP YOU

ADJECTIVE +	NOUN +	ADVENTURE/JOURNEY
BRAVE	BUNNY'S	MAGICAL QUEST
CURIOUS	CAT'S	ADVENTURES IN SPACE
HAPPY	HEDGEHOG'S	JOURNEY HOME
SILLY	DOG'S	EXPEDITION
LONELY	BEAR'S	MISSION
MAGICAL	DRAGON'S	VOYAGE
FRIENDLY	UNICORN'S	TREK
CLEVER	PRINCESS'S	ODYSSEY
PLAYFUL	PIRATE'S	SAFARI
MYSTERIOUS	WIZARD'S	PILGRIMAGE
ADORABLE	FAIRY'S	EXCURSION

A Curious Cat's Adventure in Space
The Happy Hedgehog's Journey Home

A FORMULA TO HELP YOU

ADJECTIVE	+	NOUN	+	ADVENTURE/JOURNEY
DARING		ROBOT'S		QUEST
MISCHEVIOUS		MONSTER'S		EXPEDITION
WHIMSICAL		DINOSAUR'S		JOURNEY
ENCHANTING		ELEPHANT'S		MISSION
COLOURFUL		FOX'S		ADVENTURE
JOYFUL		TURTLE'S		TREK
IMAGINATIVE		MERMAID'S		VOYAGE
EXCITING		SUPERHERO'S		PILGRIMAGE
CARING		ASTRONAUT'S		SAFARI

A FORMULA TO HELP YOU

CHARACTER'S NAME OR DESCRIPTOR	+ ACTION OR PROBLEM +	SETTING OR CONTEXT
SAMMY THE SUPER SNAIL	SAVES	THE GARDEN
ROBO-REX'S	DARING RESCUE	IN SPACE
KATIE	DISCOVERS	THE FOREST
MAX	SAVES	THE JUNGLE
LILY	EXPLORES	THE OCEAN
BEN	PROTECTS	THE DESERT
EMILY	LEARNS	OF THE CASTLE
ALEX	CONQUERS	THE MOUNTAIN
SOPHIE	OVERCOMES	THE ISLAND
JACK	IMAGINES	THE CITY
OLIVIA	DREAMS	ON THE FARM

A FORMULA TO HELP YOU

CHARACTER'S NAME OR DESCRIPTOR	➕ ACTION OR PROBLEM	➕ SETTING OR CONTEXT
CHARLIE	DREAMS	OF THE CIRCUS
EMMA	CREATES	THE SCHOOL
LUCAS	ESCAPES	WONDERLAND
MIA	FINDS	AN ENCHANTED GARDEN
NOAH	SHARES	THE MAGICAL KINGDOM
AVA	LOVES	THE FAIRYTALE LAND
ETHAN	LAUGHS	ON THE PIRATE SHIP
GRACE	PLAYS	IN THE SWEET SHOP
JACOB	GROWS	INSIDE THE SECRET HIDEOUT
ISABELLA	BELIEVES	IN THE TREEHOUSE

A FORMULA TO HELP YOU

CHARACTER'S NAME OR DESCRIPTOR +	ACTION OR PROBLEM +	THEME/OBJECT
SAMMY	AND THE	SKATEBOARD
LILY'S	-	LEMONADE STAND
MAX	AND THE	MAGICAL MIRROR
SOPHIE'S	-	SECRET GARDEN
OLIVER	AND THE	OCTOPUS ADVENTURE
EMMA'S	-	ENCHANTED FOREST
JACK'S	JOURNEY TO	JUPITER
MIA	AND THE MYSTERY	OF THE MISSING MITTENS

A FORMULA TO HELP YOU

CHARACTER'S NAME OR DESCRIPTOR	+	SETTING OR CONTEXT
FELIX THE FRIENDLY FOX'S		FOREST ADVENTURE
MIA'S MAGICAL MEADOW:		A FOREST FAIRY TALE
BENNY THE BUSY BEE'S		BIG BARN BONANZA
THE ADVENTURES OF CHARLIE THE COW		IN CLOVER CREEK
SAMMY'S SKATEBOARD SAFARI		IN THE CITY STREETS
POPPY'S PICNIC		IN THE PARK
OLIVER'S		OCEAN ODYSSEY
LEO'S		JUNGLE JOURNEY
COSMIC CODY'S CAPTIVATING		COMET QUEST
PIPPA'S POLAR BEAR PARADE:		AN ARCTIC ADVENTURE
PETAL'S PERCULIAR POTION:		A MAGICAL GARDEN ADVENTURE

YOUR TURN

Using your character's name, traits, problems they need to solve, settings etc. create 2-3 titles and then see which one is the most engaging.

Titles also help us come up with ideas we never thought of.

COLOURS, NUMBERS, SHAPES AND DAYS OF THE WEEK

COLOURS, NUMBERS, SHAPES AND DAYS OF THE WEEK

Children's stories are a great way to teach children the basics.

It's a fun way to learn things that could be seen as boring.

In your children's story, try to find ways to include numbers, or use pictures to show numbers.

'The Very Hungry Caterpillar' = counting, fruit, days of the week and colours in one go.

Have secret things (numbers, letters etc) hiding on each page and then say at the end, 'Did you notice the number 8 hiding in this book?'

CAN YOU WEAVE COLOURS INTO A STORY?

Does your book focus on one colour in particular or the rainbow?

Feature them in your pictures. You don't have to do every colour, try 2-3 or different shades of one colour and all the things that are that colour.

YOU COULD TEACH ABOUT THE COLOUR RED

FIRE TRUCK	LADYBUG	CHERRY	STOP SIGN	STRAWBERRY
TOMATO	ROSE	HEART	LIPSTICK	WATERMELON

MATCHING COLOURS WITH MOODS

Combining colours with moods is a common element in children's stories. For example: blue = sad, red = angry

Here is a list of the most common emotions that children may understand:

HAPPY	SAD	ANGRY	EXCITED	SCARED
NERVOUS	PROUD	SURPRISED	SHY	CONFUSED
BORED	SILLY	CURIOUS	LOVED	WORRIED

You could write a story based solely on an emotion or a colour?

'I am feeling a bit red today...'

You could then help your child describe what it means to feel 'red' (angry or frustrated).

NUMBERS

The benefits of including numbers in your children's story are:

BUILDING NUMERICAL LITERACY	DEVELOPING COUNTING SKILLS	TEACHING SEQUENCING AND ORDER	INTRODUCING BASIC MATHS CONCEPTS
ENCOURAGING PROBLEM-SOLVING	ENHANCING LANGUAGE DEVELOPMENT	FOSTERING CRITICAL THINKING	PROMOTING A POSITIVE ATTITUDE TOWARDS MATHS

Putting these into action:

BUILDING NUMERICAL LITERACY	"IN THE FOREST, THERE WERE THREE LITTLE BEARS EXPLORING THE WOODS."
DEVELOPING COUNTING SKILLS	"SALLY COUNTED THE COLOURFUL BALLOONS AT THE PARTY: ONE, TWO, THREE, FOUR, FIVE!"
TEACHING SEQUENCING AND ORDER	"FIRST, THE LITTLE MOUSE WOKE UP. THEN, HE BRUSHED HIS TEETH AND THEN HAD BREAKFAST."
INTRODUCING BASIC MATHS CONCEPTS	"TOM HAD THREE COOKIES, AND HIS FRIEND GAVE HIM TWO MORE. HOW MANY COOKIES DOES TOM HAVE NOW?"
ENCOURAGING PROBLEM-SOLVING	"THE FRIENDLY ANIMALS NEEDED TO CROSS THE RIVER. THEY FOUND FOUR STONES. HOW COULD THEY ARRANGE THEM TO MAKE A SAFE PATH?"

NUMBERS

You could focus your story on numbers and include a story that includes each number in a scene.

ONE	SUN	SIX	SIDES OF A HEXAGON
TWO	EYES	SEVEN	DAYS IN A WEEK
THREE	WHEELS ON A TRICYCLE	EIGHT	LEGS ON A SPIDER
FOUR	LEGS ON A CHAIR	NINE	LIVES OF A CAT
FIVE	FINGERS ON A HAND	TEN	FINGERS/TOES ON A PERSON

SHAPES

The most common shapes children will recognise are:

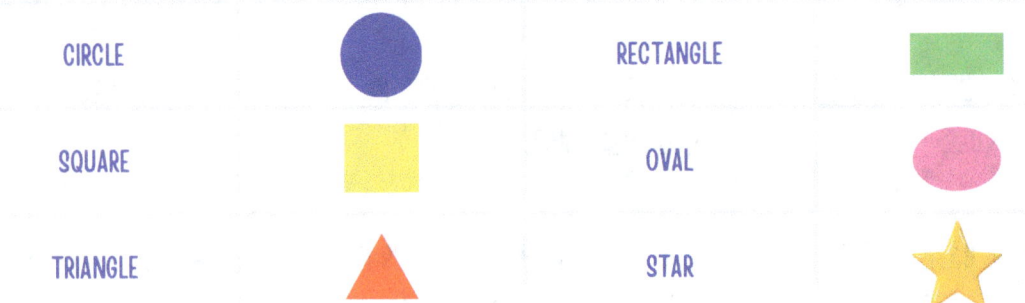

CIRCLE	RECTANGLE
SQUARE	OVAL
TRIANGLE	STAR

You can use shapes to make a story out of focusing on one shape or 2-3 different shapes.

For example, you have a main character who discovers everything that is a circle; a football, the moon, a cookie etc.

You can use repetition etc.

DAYS OF THE WEEK

Below are some activities that a child can do that correspond to each day of the week. They can be used to make a story.

MONDAY:

MAKE A MINI GARDEN BY PLANTING SEEDS IN POTS OR A SMALL PATCH OF SOIL.
MOULD CLAY INTO FUN SHAPES OR FIGURES.
MIX INGREDIENTS TO BAKE COOKIES OR MUFFINS.

TUESDAY:

TRY A NEW RECIPE WITH A PARENT OR CAREGIVER.
TAKE A NATURE WALK AND COLLECT LEAVES OR ROCKS.
TINKER WITH BUILDING BLOCKS OR LEGOS TO CREATE IMAGINATIVE STRUCTURES.

WEDNESDAY:

WATER PLANTS IN THE GARDEN OR HOUSEPLANTS INDOORS.
WATCH CLOUDS AND TRY TO IDENTIFY DIFFERENT SHAPES OR ANIMALS.
WEAVE COLOURFUL YARN OR RIBBONS INTO FRIENDSHIP BRACELETS.

THURSDAY:

TASTE DIFFERENT FRUITS OR SNACKS AND RATE THEM IN A HOMEMADE TASTE-TESTING SESSION.
TAKE A TRIP TO THE ZOO OR AQUARIUM TO OBSERVE AND LEARN ABOUT VARIOUS ANIMALS.

FRIDAY:

FLY KITES IN AN OPEN FIELD OR AT THE PARK.
FINGER PAINT ON LARGE SHEETS OF PAPER OR CARDBOARD.
FROLIC IN THE BACKYARD OR PLAYGROUND, PLAYING GAMES LIKE TAG OR HIDE-AND-SEEK.

SATURDAY:

SPLASH IN A KIDDIE POOL OR PLAY WATER GAMES IN THE BACKYARD.
SING SONGS AND PUT ON A MINI-CONCERT FOR FAMILY MEMBERS.
SEARCH FOR HIDDEN TREASURES ON A SCAVENGER HUNT OUTDOORS.

SUNDAY:

SORT TOYS OR CLOTHES TO DONATE TO THOSE IN NEED.
STORYTELLING SESSIONS WHERE CHILDREN CAN CREATE THEIR OWN TALES.
SPEND QUALITY TIME WITH FAMILY, PERHAPS HAVING A PICNIC OR PLAYING BOARD GAMES TOGETHER.

Each of the activities could be a different scene, but highlighting the letter that corresponds to the day of the week.

You could make it interactive by telling and showing the activities and then asking: 'What day of the week is it?'

They shout 'Friday!' as they have read all of the activities starting with the letter 'F'.

YOUR TURN

Think of the type of story you want to write. Educate on emotions, colours, shapes, colours etc.

Write them down here:

PART 2

WRITING YOUR STORY

REPETITION

THE 'RULE OF 3'

REPETITION

WHAT DO WE MEAN WHEN WE SAY 'REPETITION' IN CHILDREN'S STORIES?

When we refer to repetition in children's stories, we mean the intentional reuse of words, phrases, sentences, or story elements throughout the narrative.

This repetition can occur for various reasons, such as emphasising key points, aiding memory, creating rhythm and cadence, fostering predictability, engaging children interactively, and adding depth to the storytelling experience.

An example of repetition in a children's story is the classic tale of 'Goldilocks and the Three Bears.'

Throughout the story, certain phrases and events are repeated for emphasis and continuity.

For instance, the phrase "Who's been eating my porridge?" is repeated by each of the bears as they discover their belongings have been disturbed.

WHY DO CHILDREN RESPOND TO REPETITION IN STORIES?

PREDICTABILITY AND FAMILIARITY	Repetition in stories provides a sense of predictability and familiarity for children. <u>Example:</u> The repeated phrase 'Once upon a time' at the beginning of fairy tales signals to children that a story is about to start, making them feel comfortable and engaged.
MEMORY AID	Repetition helps children remember key elements of the story. <u>Example:</u> The Three Little Pigs building their houses out of straw, sticks, and bricks is a repeated sequence that helps children remember the progression of the story.
RHYTHMIC CADENCE	Repetition creates a rhythmic and melodic quality to storytelling. <u>Example:</u> The chant-like repetition of "Fee-fi-fo-fum" in 'Jack and the Beanstalk' adds excitement and anticipation to the story, captivating children with its rhythm.
INTERACTIVE ENGAGEMENT	Repetition invites children to participate in the storytelling process. <u>Example:</u> In 'The Gingerbread Man,' the repeated refrain "Run, run, as fast as you can, you can't catch me, I'm the gingerbread man!" encourages children to join in, adding to the excitement and energy of the story.

REPETITION

AN EASY WAY TO USE THE RULE OF 3.

Think of 3 obstacles – 2 things go wrong, **but the** 3rd time it goes right!

In 'Katie and the Kite,' she attempts to repair her kite 2 times in 2 different ways and it goes wrong, but on the 3rd time, she is successful!

HOW YOU CAN DO IT

Think of how to make it interesting.

Use patterned language 3 times to keep something familiar, then on the last time, make the end of that pattern something unpredictable – almost like a plot twist.

SOME EXAMPLES OF HOW REPETITION IS USED IN WRITING CHILDREN'S STORIES

CHARACTER TRAITS OR ACTIONS	**Example:** 'Bobby was happy, helpful, and always ready to share his toys.'
PROBLEM-SOLVING OR DECISION-MAKING	**Example:** 'Lily tried pushing, pulling, and finally asking for help to open the stuck door.'
DIALOGUE PATTERNS	**Example:** 'Mummy, can we go to the park? Can we go to the park? Can we go to the park?' pleaded Sarah excitedly.
DESCRIPTIVE LANGUAGE	**Example:** 'The playground was big, colourful, and filled with laughter.'
RECURRING EVENTS OR MOTIFS	**Example:** 'Every night, the stars twinkled, the moon shone, and the crickets sang their lullabies.'
LESSON REINFORCEMENT	**Example:** 'By saying "please," "thank you," and "sorry," Tommy learned that kindness makes everyone happy.'
STRUCTURAL REPETITION	**Example:** 'Every morning, Emma woke up, brushed her teeth, and gave Mommy a big hug.'

REPETITION

WHY THE RULE OF 3?

The "rule of three" is a common storytelling technique used in children's stories for its effectiveness in engaging young readers or listeners.

Here's how the rule of three helps when writing children's stories:

MEMORABILITY	Repetition of elements three times helps children remember key points or story details more easily. The repetition reinforces the information in their minds, making it more likely to stick with them.
PATTERN RECOGNITION	Children naturally gravitate towards patterns, and the rule of three creates a predictable pattern in storytelling that children find comforting and enjoyable. This pattern recognition helps them anticipate what will happen next in the story.
EMPHASIS AND IMPACT	The third occurrence of an event or phrase in the rule of three often serves as a climax or resolution, adding emphasis and impact to the story. It's a moment of culmination that can evoke strong emotions or reactions from children. <u>Example:</u> The Three Little Pigs build houses with straw, sticks, and bricks. The wolf easily blows down the first two, but the third pig's brick house withstands the strongest efforts of the wolf.
VARIETY AND PROGRESSION	By repeating elements three times, writers can introduce variations or progressions in each repetition, keeping the story dynamic and interesting. This helps maintain children's attention and curiosity throughout the narrative. <u>Example:</u> Change something small each time, but keep the same rhythm. Goldilocks tries three different bowls of porridge, finding one too hot, one too cold, and one just right. This establishes a pattern (and slight difference) of three in her interactions with the bears' belongings.

YOUR TURN

Think of your story, whether it's patterned language, repetition or obstacles. Think of what you can do 3 times, and vary them slightly and make the last one unpredictable.

Write your thoughts down here:

....
....
....
....
....
....
....
....
....
....
....
....
....
....
....

GOALS, OBSTACLES AND CONSEQUENCES

GOALS, OBSTACLES AND CONSEQUENCES

The main character's goal is what they are trying to achieve or accomplish throughout the story.

It is their motivation for taking action and drives the plot forward.

For example, in a story about a young adventurer, their goal might be to find a hidden treasure or save their village from danger.

An obstacle is something that stands in the way of the main character achieving their goal or the step towards the goal.

It creates tension and conflict in the story, driving the plot forward as the main character must overcome challenges to succeed. (Will they or won't they overcome it?)

Obstacles can take many forms, such as physical barriers, opposing characters, or internal struggles.

In the children's story 'The Lion King' by Disney, Simba faces numerous obstacles on his journey to reclaim his rightful place as king of the Pride Lands. One significant obstacle is his internal struggle with guilt and self-doubt following the death of his father, Mufasa.

Consequences are the results or outcomes of the main character's actions and decisions.

They can be positive or negative and have a direct impact on the progression of the story.

For example, if the main character makes a brave choice to confront a bully, the consequence might be that they gain confidence and earn the respect of their peers.

Conversely, if the main character acts recklessly, the consequence might be that they get into trouble or cause harm to themselves or others.

WHY IS IT GOOD TO HAVE GOALS, OBSTACLES AND CONSEQUENCES IN YOUR STORY?

ENGAGEMENT	Goals, obstacles, and consequences create an engaging storyline that captivates children's attention from start to finish.
CHARACTER DEVELOPMENT	These elements provide opportunities for characters to grow, learn, and develop important skills such as resilience and problem-solving.
REAL-LIFE LESSONS	Children learn valuable life lessons about perseverance, responsibility, and the consequences of their actions through the experiences of characters in the story.
EMPATHY AND UNDERSTANDING	Experiencing the challenges faced by characters fosters empathy and understanding, helping children appreciate diverse perspectives and experiences.
SENSE OF ACHIEVEMENT	Achieving goals and overcoming obstacles gives children a sense of satisfaction and accomplishment, boosting their confidence and self-esteem.

By incorporating goals, obstacles, and consequences into children's stories, authors create a rich and meaningful reading experience that entertains, educates, and inspires young readers.

GOALS, OBSTACLES AND CONSEQUENCES IN CHILDREN'S STORIES

THE LION, THE WITCH AND THE WARDROBE

OVERALL GOAL	The overall goal of 'The Lion, the Witch, and the Wardrobe' is to defeat the White Witch and restore peace and prosperity to the magical land of Narnia.
GOAL	Defeat the White Witch and restore peace to Narnia.
STEP 1	Entering Narnia.
OBSTACLE	The Pevensie siblings must navigate the dangers of Narnia and face the oppressive rule of the White Witch.
CONSEQUENCES	They join forces with Narnian creatures to overthrow the Witch.
STEP 2	Joining the Resistance.
OBSTACLE	The siblings encounter resistance from the Witch's army as they seek support from Aslan.
CONSEQUENCES	They learn about courage and friendship on their journey.
STEP 3	The Final Battle.
OBSTACLE	The White Witch summons her forces to defend her reign.
CONSEQUENCES	The siblings bravely confront the Witch, leading to victory and peace in Narnia.

GOALS, OBSTACLES AND CONSEQUENCES

One top tip for setting goals, obstacles and consequences in your story is to have questions in mind.

Will my main character achieve their mission?

Yes, by using all the resources available they will achieve their mission.

What is your story's question and answer?

Answering this question will help you with your character's journey.

Write it as a paragraph to get the information out of your head. Think about what their journey will be like.

OUR EXAMPLE –
KATIE AND THE KITE

QUESTION	Will Katie's kite fly?
WILL MY MAIN CHARACTER ACHIEVE THEIR MISSION?	Yes, by using all the resources available, making sure it is repaired, and if there is enough wind, Katie will achieve her mission.
HER MAIN GOAL	To fly her kite.
THE OBSTACLES ARE	It is damaged and there isn't enough wind.
PLOT TWIST	She meets a friend and the kite comes back to her.
ENDING	(Answers the question) Katie flies her kite and makes a friend.

MAKE YOU OBSTACLES SOMETHING THAT COULD BE THE WORST THING TO HAPPEN AT THAT TIME.

A SELECTION OF GOALS

FINDING A LOST TREASURE OR ARTEFACT

RESCUING A KIDNAPPED FRIEND OR FAMILY MEMBER

WINNING A COMPETITION OR CONTEST

MAKING NEW FRIENDS OR FITTING IN AT A NEW SCHOOL

OVERCOMING A PERSONAL FEAR OR OBSTACLE

SAVING A MAGICAL KINGDOM OR WORLD FROM DESTRUCTION

LEARNING A NEW SKILL OR MASTERING A CHALLENGE

REUNITING WITH A LOST LOVED ONE OR PET

DISCOVERING THE TRUTH BEHIND A MYSTERY OR SECRET

FINDING THEIR WAY BACK HOME AFTER GETTING LOST

A SELECTION OF OBSTACLES

A LOCKED DOOR BLOCKING THE PROTAGONIST'S PATH

GETTING LOST IN A MAZE OR UNFAMILIAR TERRAIN

FACING A BULLY AT SCHOOL

FORGETTING AN IMPORTANT ITEM NEEDED TO COMPLETE A TASK

FEELING NERVOUS BEFORE A PERFORMANCE OR PRESENTATION

LOSING A GAME OR COMPETITION

GETTING CAUGHT IN THE RAIN WITHOUT AN UMBRELLA

DROPPING AND BREAKING A VALUABLE OBJECT

HAVING A DISAGREEMENT WITH A FRIEND

MISSING THE BUS OR TRAIN TO AN IMPORTANT EVENT

BEING PURSUED BY A WILD ANIMAL OR MONSTER

DEALING WITH A SUDDEN ILLNESS OR INJURY

A SELECTION OF CONSEQUENCES

LEARNING AN IMPORTANT LESSON OR MORAL

GAINING A NEW SKILL OR PERSPECTIVE

FORMING STRONGER BONDS WITH FRIENDS OR FAMILY

OVERCOMING FEAR OR SELF-DOUBT

GROWING IN CONFIDENCE AND RESILIENCE

FACING REPERCUSSIONS FOR THEIR ACTIONS

EXPERIENCING A CHANGE IN THEIR CIRCUMSTANCES OR ENVIRONMENT

FINDING UNEXPECTED OPPORTUNITIES OR SOLUTIONS

FACING DISAPPOINTMENT OR SETBACKS

ACHIEVING SUCCESS OR REACHING THEIR GOAL

SUFFERING PHYSICAL INJURIES THAT REQUIRE TIME TO HEAL

EXPERIENCING A CHANGE IN THEIR RELATIONSHIPS WITH OTHER CHARACTERS

GAINING A DEEPER UNDERSTANDING OF THEMSELVES AND THEIR STRENGTHS

MAKING AMENDS FOR MISTAKES OR WRONGDOINGS THEY MADE DURING THEIR JOURNEY

GOALS, OBSTACLES AND CONSEQUENCES

YOUR TURN – Overall

TITLE:

QUESTION	
WILL MY MAIN CHARACTER ACHIEVE THEIR MISSION?	
MAIN GOAL	
THE OBSTACLES ARE	
PLOT TWIST IDEA?	
ENDING	

MAKE YOU OBSTACLES SOMETHING THAT COULD BE THE WORST THING TO HAPPEN AT THAT TIME.

YOUR TURN

Fill in the blanks for your story.

TITLE	
THEME	
MAIN CHARACTER	
GOAL	
WHAT IS THE QUESTION?	
1ST OBSTACLE TO THE GOAL	
CONSEQUENCE	
2ND OBSTACLE TO THE GOAL	
CONSEQUENCE	
3RD OBSTACLE TO THE GOAL	
CONSEQUENCE	
PLOT TWIST	
ENDING	
DOES THE ENDING ANSWER THE ORIGINAL QUESTION?	

THE INCITING EVENT

THE INCITING EVENT

The inciting event in a children's story is the event that sets the plot in motion and introduces the main conflict or problem that the characters must face. Here are some ideas for inciting events in children's stories:

DISCOVERY OF A MYSTERIOUS OBJECT	The main character discovers a mysterious object, like a treasure map, a magical artefact, or a lost toy, setting off an adventure to uncover its secrets.
ENCOUNTER WITH A NEW FRIEND OR CREATURE	The main character encounters a new friend or creature with a problem or dilemma, sparking a quest to help them solve it and learn valuable lessons along the way.
UNEXPECTED INVITATION OR CHALLENGE	The main character receives an unexpected invitation to a competition, talent show, or challenge, igniting their determination to participate and succeed.
CHANGE IN THE ENVIRONMENT OR ROUTINE	The main character experiences a sudden change in their environment or routine, such as moving to a new house, starting a new school year, or encountering a strange phenomenon, leading to unexpected adventures and discoveries.
DISAPPEARANCE OF SOMETHING IMPORTANT	Something important to the main character, like a beloved pet, a family heirloom, or a magical object, disappears mysteriously, prompting a search mission to retrieve it and restore balance.

START WITH ACTION!

THE INCITING EVENT

ENCOUNTER WITH A PROBLEMATIC SITUATION	The main character encounters a problematic situation in their community, like pollution in the park, bullying at school, or a mystery to solve, inspiring them to take action and make a positive difference.
UNEXPECTED VISITOR	An unexpected visitor arrives in the main character's life, such as a visitor from another planet, a lost traveller, or a mysterious stranger, bringing with them a message or quest that propels the story forward.
ACCIDENTAL ACTIVATION OF MAGIC OR POWERS	The main character accidentally activates a magical ability or power they didn't know they had, leading to unforeseen consequences and adventures as they learn to control their newfound abilities.
RACE AGAINST TIME	The main character discovers they only have a limited amount of time to achieve a goal or complete a task, like finding a lost treasure before it's gone forever or saving a friend from a curse before it's too late.
DREAM OR VISION OF THE FUTURE	The main character has a dream or vision of the future that reveals a looming threat or challenge, motivating them to take action to prevent it from happening.

START WITH ACTION!

PLOT TWISTS AND ENDINGS

PLOT TWISTS AND ENDINGS

A plot twist is a sudden and unexpected change or development in the storyline that alters the course of events or challenges the audience's expectations.

Example: In 'The Wizard of Oz' by L. Frank Baum, the revelation that the Wizard is just an ordinary man behind a curtain is a significant plot twist.

This unexpected revelation changes the characters' perceptions of the Wizard and reshapes their journey.

The ending of a story refers to the conclusion or resolution of the plot, where loose ends are tied up, and the fate of the characters is revealed.

Example: In 'Charlotte's Web' by E.B. White, the ending where Wilbur's friend Charlotte dies but leaves behind her spiderlings and her message of friendship engraved in her web is a poignant and memorable conclusion.

This ending brings closure to the story while leaving a lasting impact on readers about the power of friendship and sacrifice.

Endings are massively important.

Think of a joke.

You wouldn't start writing a joke before knowing the punchline would you?

HOW TO WRITE A GOOD PLOT TWIST AND ENDING

- Surprise and engagement: Keep young readers engaged with unexpected twists and turns.

- Emotional impact: Endings should leave a strong emotional impression, while plot twists should spark curiosity and imagination.

- Reinforce themes: Ensure that endings and plot twists reinforce the story's themes and lessons for young readers

PLOT TWISTS AND ENDINGS

You know what your character wants to achieve (their goal), so do they achieve it?

How?

- Make how or what happens in the end unpredictable or fun.

- Think of what the audience would be expecting and do the opposite.

Why not end with a question? This gets your audience thinking and talking about it. 'What will that wish be?' could be an example of ending with a question to a story relevant to this theme.

Endings should be happy or uplifting and should help spread the message (theme) of the story.

Try to avoid ambiguous endings.

Make them definitive.

Your ending must solve the original problem.

In 'Katie and the Kite,' Katie wanted to a) make a friend and b) wanted her kite to fly.

The main character must solve the problem or have a big part to play.

The main character must evolve in some way by the end of the story.

WHEN SHOULD A PLOT TWIST OCCUR IN A STORY?

A plot twist in a children's story should occur strategically, ideally at the midpoint or just before a climactic moment.

For example, in 'Harry Potter and the Philosopher's Stone,' the plot twist happens near the end when Harry realises Professor Snape is not the villain he thought he was.

PLOT TWISTS AND ENDINGS

IDEAS FOR YOUR PLOT TWISTS

FRIENDLY MONSTER	A scary monster turns out to be friendly and playful.
MISSING TOY	A lost toy is found hiding in plain sight.
TALKING ANIMAL	An animal surprises by being able to talk.
MAGICAL TRANSFORMATION	Something ordinary transforms into something magical at the right/wrong time.
SURPRISE GUEST	An unexpected guest brings excitement and adventure.
REVERSE ROLE	The hero needs rescuing, and a minor character saves the day.
HIDDEN TREASURE	An ordinary object holds a secret treasure.
SILLY MIX-UP	Amusing misunderstandings lead to unexpected outcomes.
MYSTERIOUS VISITOR	A mysterious package sets off a thrilling adventure.
UNLIKELY FRIENDSHIP	A friendship forms between unlikely characters.

PLOT TWISTS AND ENDINGS

IDEAS FOR YOUR ENDINGS

HAPPY ENDING	Characters achieve their goals and find joy.
UNEXPECTED TWIST	A surprise revelation changes everything.
OPEN-ENDED CONCLUSION	Leaves room for imagination.
LESSON LEARNED	Characters reflect and grow.
BITTERSWEET ENDING	Mixed emotions but resolution.
RETURN TO NORMALCY	Characters back home, changed.
CIRCLE OF FRIENDSHIP	Unity and acceptance celebrated.
HEROIC TRIUMPH	Protagonist overcomes fear and wins.
MAGICAL TRANSFORMATION	Ends with wonder and possibility.
RESOLUTION THROUGH FRIENDSHIP	Characters bond, solving problems together.

YOUR TURN

Pick some ideas for a plot twist and an ending.

Mix and match and see which one is the MOST unpredictable.

WRITING YOUR STORY STRUCTURE

STRUCTURE

A children's story structure is the framework of a narrative, including characters, setting, plot development, climax, and resolution, and is designed to engage young readers and convey meaningful messages.

THE BENEFITS OF USING A STRUCTURE

Using a structure for children's stories helps to organise ideas, create engaging characters and plotlines, and make the story easier to follow and enjoy for young readers.

The plot is your story structure. It's as important as your characters. You want your plot to be engaging and yet unpredictable - keep them guessing.

How do we do this?

Make things go wrong... really wrong.

Play on your characters' fears and make them happen.

Make them have obstacles in the way.

You want your readers to say, 'Will they or won't they get through this?' in their head.

Think of your plot as beginning, middle and end.

Your beginning should be a quarter of your story and your end should be a quarter, the 'action' is in the middle. These are the steps and the obstacles.

Think of what your character wants, and what steps they need to take to get it.

Make things go wrong. Make it worse before it gets better.

A good idea for an ending is to make it the opposite of the beginning and or to solve the initial problem.

This makes your story exciting...

STRUCTURE

If your character needs to fly a damaged kite (GOAL) (like in our story 'Katie and the Kite'), this is what needs to happen:

STEP 1	Fix damage to the kite.
OBSTACLE	The kite didn't work well enough.
CONSEQUENCE	Katie needs to find better materials to fix it with.
STEP 2	Katie tries again.
OBSTACLE	There's no wind.
CONSEQUENCE	Katie gets disheartened and has to wait for wind.

WHAT HAPPENS IF YOU WRITE WITHOUT A STRUCTURE?

Without a structure, a children's story can feel confusing and disjointed, making it hard for young readers to follow and engage with the plot.

It may also fail to effectively convey its message, resulting in a less compelling reading experience.

A plan will help you know where you're headed – it stops you wandering off.

Know your ending before you start writing your story.

STRUCTURE

Here is an example of a structure in action – let's use 'The Lion, The Witch and The Wardrobe' again:

INTRODUCTION TO MAIN CHARACTER	We meet the Pevensie siblings – Peter, Susan, Edmund, and Lucy – who are sent to the countryside during World War II for safety.
INTRODUCE PROBLEM	The children feel bored and isolated in the old Professor's mansion.
INCITING EVENT (WHAT DOES THE MAIN CHARACTER NEED TO DO AND WHY)	Lucy, the youngest, discovers a magical wardrobe in a spare room and enters it, leading to the land of Narnia. She needs to find a way back home because she's frightened and alone.
THEIR OVERALL GOAL	The siblings want to explore Narnia and understand its mysteries while finding a way to return home safely.
STEP 1 TO ACHIEVE THAT GOAL	Lucy returns to the wardrobe to tell her siblings about Narnia and convince them it's real.
OBSTACLE TO THAT	Edmund doesn't believe Lucy and mocks her, causing tension among the siblings.
CONSEQUENCE	The siblings argue and doubt each other's trustworthiness.

STRUCTURE

STEP 2 TO ACHIEVE THAT GOAL	Lucy insists on returning to Narnia to prove its existence to her siblings.
OBSTACLE TO THAT	Edmund follows Lucy into Narnia but gets separated from her.
CONSEQUENCE	Edmund encounters the White Witch, who manipulates him and threatens Narnia's safety.
PLOT TWIST	The children learn about the prophecy of the four thrones and their roles as kings and queens of Narnia.
STEP 3 TO ACHIEVE THAT GOAL	The siblings unite to overthrow the White Witch and restore peace to Narnia.
OBSTACLE TO THAT	They face the White Witch's army and the treacherous terrain of Narnia.
CONSEQUENCE	Peter, Susan, Edmund, and Lucy risk their lives but ultimately defeat the White Witch with the help of Aslan.
ENDING/RESOLUTION	The siblings become the rulers of Narnia, fulfilling the prophecy. They bring prosperity and joy to the land while learning valuable lessons about courage, sacrifice, and family bonds. Eventually, they return to the real world, having grown wiser and stronger from their adventures in Narnia.

YOUR TURN

You may not be able to fill it all in yet – but do as much as you can.

INTRODUCTION TO MAIN CHARACTER	
INTRODUCE PROBLEM	
INCITING EVENT (WHAT DOES THE MAIN CHARACTER NEED TO DO AND WHY)	
THEIR OVERALL GOAL	
STEP 1 TO ACHIEVE THAT GOAL	
OBSTACLE TO THAT	
CONSEQUENCE	

YOUR TURN

STEP 2 TO ACHIEVE THAT GOAL	
OBSTACLE TO THAT	
CONSEQUENCE	
PLOT TWIST	
STEP 3 TO ACHIEVE THAT GOAL	
OBSTACLE TO THAT	
CONSEQUENCE	
ENDING/RESOLUTION	

THE CONTENT: LANGUAGE

SATPIN

SATPIN

SATPIN is an acronym used in phonics education to represent the initial consonant sounds of six commonly taught letters: S, A, T, P, I, and N.

SATPIN are the first six letters and sounds your child will learn when they start reading. Teachers start with these sounds because they're very common and they make blending and segmenting, as well as reading and spelling, far easier.

These letters are often among the first introduced to children when they begin learning phonics and reading skills.

These letters are among the first taught in phonics because they are used to form many simple, frequently encountered words in English

By mastering the sounds and words associated with SATPIN, children can build a strong foundation for further phonics instruction and literacy development.

These letters make up words like "sat," "ant," and "pan," which are easy for children to recognise and sound out.

Mastering these letters helps children start reading on their own.

SATPIN

HOW DO YOU USE SATPIN?

When SATPIN letters are put together you can blend and segment them to read and write several simple words – SAT – SIT – PAN – PAT- PIN –TIP – TAP – ANT – SAP etc. If you just teach children in the order of the alphabet, they would not be able to make as many simple words initially.

The words below are all SATPIN words.

Can you make a story out of them?

SUN, APPLE, TREE, PIG, IGLOO AND NET

What about...

Once upon a sunny day, a friendly pig named Peter decided to explore the farm. He trotted to a big tree where he found a delicious apple hanging from a branch. As he reached for it, he spotted something unusual nearby – an igloo made of ice! It has blown there from there from Greenland!

Curious, Peter waddled closer and found a polar bear named Percy inside, who was caught in a fishing net where he tried to catch his dinner. Peter has to try and help free Percy the polar bear and get him back home. They played together under the warm sun, enjoying the tasty apple before Percy had to return to Greenland.

WHY IS THIS IMPORTANT FOR YOU?

Think of how you can use the SATPIN letters and words in your story to help children develop.

Can you use the words for your title, main character, setting etc.?

SATPIN RHYMING WORDS

S
- SUN: FUN, RUN, BUN
- SAND: BAND, HAND, LAND
- SOCK: ROCK, CLOCK, DOCK
- SNAKE: CAKE, LAKE, RAKE
- STAR: CAR, FAR, JAR

A
- APPLE: GRAPPLE
- ANT: PANT
- ACORN: UNICORN, CORN, TORN
- ARROW: SPARROW, NARROW, BARROW

T
- TURTLE: HURTLE, MYRTLE, GIRDLE
- TRAIN: RAIN, LANE, SPAIN
- TOOTH: BOOTH, YOUTH, RUTH
- TREE: BEE, FREE, THREE

P
- PIG: FIG, WIG, DIG

I
- INSECT: CORRECT, AFFECT, CONNECT
- IGGY: ZIGGY, TWIGGY, PIGGY

N
- NOSE: ROSE, POSE, CLOSE
- NEST: BEST, REST, TEST
- NET: BET, GET, SET
- NUT: HUT, GUT, CUT
- NAP: CAP, LAP, MAP

PHONICS

PHONICS

Phonics in early years refers to the method of teaching children to read by associating sounds with letters or groups of letters.

A story might introduce characters or objects whose names begin with the same sound, such as "Sam the snake" or "Teddy the tiger."

Stories that include rhymes help children recognise similar sound patterns, such as "cat," "bat," and "hat."

Understanding phonics can help when writing children's stories.

Use simple words that match sounds, like "cat" and "bat."

Repeating sounds, like "buzz" and "pop," also help children learn phonics.

WHAT WORDS SHOULD I USE TO HELP CHILDREN WITH PHONICS?

Short letters and long letters in phonics refer to the duration of the vowel sound in a word. Short letters produce short vowel sounds, while long letters produce long vowel sounds.
For example:

- Short "a" sounds: like in "cat," "bat," and "cap."
- Long "a" sounds: like in "cake," "take," and "make."

WHY SHOULD WE USE THESE WORDS IN OUR STORY?

Using short and long vowel words in children's stories helps reinforce phonics and supports early reading skills, making the reading experience more engaging and enjoyable for young readers.

VOWEL PATTERNS - PHONETIC WORD LIST

VOWEL PATTERN	WORD EXAMPLES
SHORT 'a'	FAN, PAN, MAN, CAT, RAT, BAT, HAT, MAT, MAD, BAD, TAG, DAD, CAN, MAN.
SHORT 'e'	PEN, TEN, WHEN, BET, LET, JET, BED, TED, MEN, GET, MET, WED, RED, HEN.
SHORT 'i'	BIT, PIT, FIT, FIN, WIN, PIN, LIT, JIG, HIT, MIX, BIG, DIG, PIILL, MIT, WIT, DIN.
SHORT 'o'	POT, LOT, DOT, HOP, SHOP, DROP, TOP, BOX, HOG, FROG, TOG, POP, MOP, COP.
SHORT 'u'	FUN, RUN, SUN, BUN, UP, CUP, BUG, RUG, HUG, MUG, CUT, NUT, HUT, GUM, JUG.
LONG 'a'	FAIL, RAIN, PAIL, TALE, WHALE, MALE, CAKE, LAKE, TAKE, MAKE, RAKE, NAME.
LONG 'e'	FEET, SHEEP, KEEP, HEAT, MEAT, BEAT, BEE, FREE, DEEP, SEED, GREEN, STREET.
LONG 'i'	CRIED, PIE, FILES, FILE, MILE, PILE, BIKE, NINE, TIME, SHINE, LINE, SLIDE, FIRE.
LONG 'o'	BOAT, COAT, FLOAT, BONE, CONE, NOTE, PHONE, HOME, NOSE, ROSE, POKE, ROPE.
LONG 'u'	BLUE, CLUE, TRUE, CUTE, CUBE, TUBE, MUTE, FLUTE, DUNE, USE, MULE, JUNE.

ALLITERATION

ALLITERATION

Alliteration in children's stories refers to the repetition of consonant sounds at the beginning of neighbouring words.

Its purpose is to create rhythm, emphasis, and musicality in the text, making the story more engaging and memorable for young readers.

EXAMPLES OF ALLITERATION

Silly Sally sells seashells by the seashore.

Peter Piper picked a peck of pickled peppers.

Five fat frogs frolicked in the pond.

The big brown bear bakes bread in the barn.

Cindy the cat caught a curious cricket.

Sammy the snake slithered silently through the grass.

Gus the goat grazed on green grass.

Alliteration helps develop language skills and phonemic awareness in young readers. It enhances storytelling and makes reading enjoyable for children while improving their language skills and memory retention.

When writing, ensure you choose keywords with the same initial consonant sound, find similar words, and use them to create catchy phrases.

Ensure the alliteration fits naturally into the story and read aloud to check the flow.

YOUR TURN

Write 3-5 sentences for your story using alliteration.

Using your main character's name is an easy start.

ONOMATOPOEIA

ONOMATOPOEIA

Onomatopoeia in writing children's stories refers to words that imitate the sound they represent, enhancing sensory experiences within the narrative.

The use of onomatopoeia adds excitement to children's stories by bringing sounds to life. It engages young readers, stimulates their imagination, and helps them connect with the story on a sensory level, making the reading experience more immersive and enjoyable.

EXAMPLES OF ONOMATOPOEIA	
BUZZ	THE SOUND OF A BEE.
ROAR	THE SOUND OF A LION.
SPLASH	THE SOUND OF WATER.
CRUNCH	THE SOUND OF BITING INTO SOMETHING CRISP.
HISS	THE SOUND OF A SNAKE.
BOOM	THE SOUND OF THUNDER.
DING-DONG	THE SOUND OF A DOORBELL.
SIZZLE	THE SOUND OF FRYING FOOD.
POP	THE SOUND OF A BALLOON BURSTING.
WHIZZ	THE SOUND OF SOMETHING MOVING QUICKLY.

ONOMATOPOEIA

Onomatopoeia in writing children's stories creates:

- Engagement: Onomatopoeia makes stories exciting and immersive for kids by bringing sounds to life.

- Imagination: Kids enjoy vivid imagery and sensory stimulation from onomatopoeia, enhancing their enjoyment of the story.

- Interactive reading: Onomatopoeia encourages kids to participate in the story by making sound effects themselves.

EXAMPLES OF ONOMATOPOEIA IN STORIES

The bees buzzed around the blooming flowers in the garden.

The doorbell went ding-dong as guests arrived for the party.

With a sizzle and a pop, the bacon cooked in the frying pan.

The rain pitter-pattered against the window on a stormy night.

ONOMATOPOEIA

EXAMPLES OF ONOMATOPOEIA

BANG (LOUD NOISE)	BOOM (EXPLOSION)	CRASH (COLLISION)
POP (BURSTING)	SNAP (BREAKING)	CRACK (FRACTURING)
CLANG (METAL HITTING)	DING-DONG (BELL RINGING)	THUMP (HEAVY IMPACT)
HISS (SNAKE)	THUD (DULL IMPACT)	WHACK (SHARP BLOW)
ROAR (LION)	GROWL (ANGRY ANIMAL)	MEOW (CAT)
BARK (DOG)	WOOF (DOG)	RIBBIT (FROG)
QUACK (DUCK)	MOO (COW)	OINK (PIG)
BAA (SHEEP)	NEIGH (HORSE)	TWEET (BIRD)
CHIRP (BIRD)	HOOT (OWL)	CAW (CROW)
SQUEAK (HIGH-PITCHED)	SCREECH (LOUD, HIGH-PITCHED)	WHISTLE (BLOWING AIR)
BUZZ (CONTINUOUS BUZZING)	HUM (LOW, CONTINUOUS)	BEEP (ELECTRONIC)
HONK (CAR HORN)	VROOM (ENGINE)	ZOOM (FAST MOVEMENT)
SQUAWK (LOUD, HARSH CRY)	SNORT (ANIMAL BREATHING)	PURR (CONTENTED CAT)

ONOMATOPOEIA

EXAMPLES OF ONOMATOPOEIA

GRUNT (ANIMAL NOISE)	CLUCK (CHICKEN)	RUMBLE (LOW, CONTINUOUS)
RUSTLE (MOVEMENT OF LEAVES)	SWISH (FAST MOVEMENT THROUGH AIR)	SLURP (DRINKING SOUND)
GULP (SWALLOWING)	CHEW (BITING AND GRINDING)	SMACK (SHARP NOISE)
SIZZLE (COOKING SOUND)	FIZZLE (FADING OUT)	SPLASH (WATER)
DRIP (FALLING LIQUID)	GUSH (BURST OF LIQUID)	TRICKLE (SLOW LIQUID FLOW)
SPLOSH (SLOSHING LIQUID)	SLURP (DRINKING)	GLUG (DRINKING)
SWISH (FAST MOVEMENT)	SWIRL (CIRCULAR MOTION)	WHIRL (RAPID SPINNING)
WHOOSH (FAST MOVEMENT)	SLOSH (SLOSHING LIQUID)	SLAP (SHARP IMPACT)
CLAP (HANDS)	TINKLE (LIGHT, METALLIC SOUND)	TWINKLE (FAINT, HIGH SOUND)
RUSTLE (GENTLE MOVEMENT)	CRACKLE (SHARP, CRACKLING SOUND)	PLOP (SOFT, HEAVY SOUND)
GIGGLE (LIGHT, HAPPY SOUND)	MUNCH (EATING)	SNORE (SLEEPING SOUND)
SNIGGER (MOCKING LAUGHTER)	SHUDDER (SHAKING FROM FEAR)	SHIVER (SHAKING FROM COLD)

USING ONOMATOPOEIA IN YOUR WRITING

DING-DONG	DING-DONG! THE DOORBELL CHIMED AS THE VISITOR ARRIVED.
TOOT-TOOT	THE TOY TRAIN WENT 'TOOT-TOOT' AS IT CHUGGED ALONG THE TRACKS.
WHEE	"WHEE!" SARAH GIGGLED AS SHE SLID DOWN THE SLIDE.
BOOP	SHE GAVE THE PUPPY'S NOSE A LITTLE 'BOOP' AND IT LICKED HER HAND.
MUNCH	THE CHILDREN SAT IN THE CINEMA, MUNCHING ON THEIR POPCORN.
PLOP	THE PEBBLE MADE A SOFT 'PLOP' AS IT DROPPED INTO THE POND.
DRIP-DROP	OUTSIDE THE WINDOW, THEY COULD HEAR THE 'DRIP-DROP' OF RAIN.
WHACK	HE GAVE THE BALL A 'WHACK' WITH HIS BAT, SENDING IT FLYING.
YIPPEE	"YIPPEE!" THE CHILDREN CHEERED AS THEY REACHED THE TOP OF THE HILL.
GULP	WITH A NERVOUS 'GULP', SHE TOOK A SIP OF HER LEMONADE.
HURRAY	HURRAY! THE TEAM WON THE GAME AND THE CROWD ERUPTED IN CHEERS.
CRUNCHY	THE LEAVES UNDERFOOT MADE A 'CRUNCHY' SOUND AS THEY WALKED THROUGH THE FOREST.
SHUSH	"SHUSH!" THE LIBRARIAN WHISPERED AS THE CHILDREN ENTERED THE LIBRARY.

USING ONOMATOPOEIA IN YOUR WRITING

SHIMMER	THE LEAVES SHIMMERED IN THE BREEZE, MAKING A GENTLE SOUND.
HUSH	"HUSH, LITTLE ONE, IT'S TIME TO GO TO SLEEP," WHISPERED THE PARENT.
CLATTER	THE POTS AND PANS MADE A LOUD 'CLATTER' AS THEY FELL TO THE FLOOR.
FLUTTER	THE BUTTERFLY FLUTTERED BY, ITS WINGS MAKING A SOFT SOUND.
WIGGLE	THE WORM BEGAN TO WIGGLE AND SQUIRM IN THE SOIL.
GIGGLE	THE CHILDREN COULDN'T HELP BUT GIGGLE AT THE FUNNY JOKE.
HICCUP	HE LET OUT A LITTLE 'HICCUP' AFTER DRINKING HIS SODA TOO QUICKLY.
SQUEAL	THE CHILDREN LET OUT A SQUEAL OF DELIGHT WHEN THEY SAW THE BALLOONS.
ZING	THE ARROW FLEW THROUGH THE AIR WITH A 'ZING', HITTING THE TARGET.
SWOOP	THE OWL SWOOPED DOWN FROM THE TREE, ITS WINGS SILENT IN THE NIGHT.
TWINKLE	THE STARS BEGAN TO TWINKLE IN THE NIGHT SKY, THEIR LIGHT FLICKERING GENTLY.
ZIP	HE PULLED THE ZIPPER UP ON HIS JACKET WITH A 'ZIP.'
WHIZ	THE ARROW WHIZZED PAST, NARROWLY MISSING ITS TARGET.
TWANG	THE MUSICIAN PLUCKED THE GUITAR STRING, PRODUCING A TWANGY SOUND.

YOUR TURN

Using your imagination and the lists on the previous pages, come up with some sentences using onomatopoeia.

Think of 1-2 scenes in your potential story and write them using onomatopoeia.

Write them down here:

SIMILES

SIMILES

Similes are figures of speech that compare two different things using the words "like" or "as." They are used to make descriptions more vivid and engaging by drawing parallels between the characteristics of the two things being compared.

Examples of similes in children's stories:

Description of a character:

- "Her hair was as shiny as a polished mirror."
- "He was as brave as a lion when facing his fears."

Description of weather:

- "The rain fell like tears from the sky."
- "The wind howled like a pack of wolves on a winter night."

Description of actions:

- "She danced as gracefully as a butterfly fluttering in the breeze."
- "He ran as fast as a cheetah chasing its prey."

Description of size or shape:

- "The pumpkin was round like a full moon."
- "The tree stretched its branches high into the sky like a giant reaching for the stars."

EXAMPLES OF SIMILES

AS BRAVE AS A LION	AS BUSY AS A BEE	AS LIGHT AS A FEATHER	AS BIG AS A BEAR
AS CUTE AS A BUTTON	AS STRONG AS AN OX	AS FAST AS A CHEETAH	AS SMALL AS A MOUSE
AS BRIGHT AS THE SUN	AS SWEET AS CANDY	AS BUSY AS ANTS	AS CLEAN AS A WHISTLE
AS SHINY AS A STAR	AS QUICK AS LIGHTNING	AS HAPPY AS A CLAM	AS HUNGRY AS A WOLF
AS SMOOTH AS SILK	AS SOFT AS A PILLOW	AS TALL AS A TREE	AS SHINY AS A DIAMOND
AS PLAYFUL AS A PUPPY	AS COLOURFUL AS A RAINBOW	AS LOUD AS THUNDER	AS SLOW AS A SNAIL
AS COSY AS A BLANKET	AS SMART AS A FOX	AS BRAVE AS A SUPERHERO	AS COLD AS SNOW
AS HAPPY AS A CLOWN	AS CURIOUS AS A CAT	AS SLIPPERY AS AN EEL	AS FAST AS A ROCKET
AS TASTY AS A TREAT	AS SMOOTH AS BUTTER	AS QUIET AS A MOUSE	AS QUIET AS A WHISPER
AS BOUNCY AS A BALL	AS COLD AS ICE	AS HOT AS THE SUN	AS BIG AS A HOUSE
AS BRIGHT AS A RAINBOW	AS BRAVE AS A PIRATE	AS WARM AS A HUG	AS SLIPPERY AS A FISH

SYLLABLES

SYLLABLES

Syllables are the beats or sounds in a word.

When writing a children's story, understanding syllables helps in creating words that are easy to pronounce and understand for young readers.

Each syllable usually contains a vowel sound and can help children learn to sound out words while reading.

HOW MANY SYLLABLES?

In an early years story, it's common to use words with one or two syllables.

This helps keep the text simple and easy for young readers to understand and pronounce.

However, there may be occasional words with three syllables, but they are typically limited to avoid overwhelming young readers.

1-SYLLABLE WORDS	2-SYLLABLE WORDS	3-SYLLABLE WORDS
CAT	RA-BBIT	BA-NA-NA
DOG	TI-GER	EL-E-PHANT
HAT	A-PPLE	BUT-TER-FLY
SUN	FL-OWER	UM-BR-ELLA
FISH	BU-NNY	CAS-U-AL

WHERE YOU CAN, LIMIT THE AMOUNT OF 3 SYLLABLE WORDS IN AN EARLY YEARS STORY.

SYLLABLES

HOW CAN WE USE SYLLABLES IN OUR STORY TO MAKE IT MORE INTERESTING?

To make your story more interesting with syllables, vary the length of words.

Short words can create a quick pace, while longer ones slow things down.

Use this to build tension, show emotions, or highlight important points. It's a simple way to keep readers engaged and add depth to your writing.

Your picture book is meant to be read aloud – to a class or to your own children/relatives.

Use simple, straightforward language.

What you don't want is having to keep stopping to explain the words – it loses the flow of the story. Words that are 3+ syllables 'could' be too complex in some cases.

If you repeat words, they will learn them and hear them in context.

Don't use complicated ways to describe things.

Pictures help with that. Use attractive sounding words 'glittery, sparkly' etc. You don't have to use rhyme.

This is where your story can help educate while they are engrossed in the story.

Feel free to make up words too.

Julia Donaldson had the 'Smeds and the Smoos' (one planet was red and the other was blue).

SYLLABLES

SYLLABLE	EXAMPLES
/a/ (as in 'apple')	CAT, HAT, MAT
/b/ (as in 'ball')	TALL, CALL, FALL
/c/ (as in 'cat')	RAT, BAT, SAT
/d/ (as in 'dog')	FROG, LOG, JOG
/e/ (as in 'egg')	LEG, PEG, BEG
/f/ (as in 'fish')	DISH, WISH, FISH
/g/ (as in 'goat')	COAT, BOAT, FLOAT
/h/ (as in 'hat')	BAT, RAT, MAT
/i/ (as in 'igloo')	PIG, FIG, WIG
/j/ (as in 'jump')	BUMP, JUMP, LUMP
/k/ (as in 'kite')	BITE, LIGHT, NIGHT
/l/ (as in 'lion')	MILE, TILE, SMILE
/m/ (as in 'monkey')	KEY, TREE, FREE

SYLLABLES

SYLLABLE	EXAMPLES
/n/ (as in 'nest')	BEST, REST, VEST
/o/ (as in 'octopus')	POT, DOT, HOT
/p/ (as in 'pig')	DIG, BIG, FIG
/q/ (as in 'queen')	SEEN, MEAN, GREEN
/r/ (as in 'rabbit')	CAB, GRAB, SLAB
/s/ (as in 'snake')	LAKE, CAKE, MAKE
/t/ (as in 'tat')	BAT, RAT, MAT
/u/ (as in 'umbrella')	BUS, GUS, PLUS
/v/ (as in 'violin')	BIN, WIN, THIN
/w/ (as in 'wagon')	MEN, PEN, TEN
/x/ (as in 'box')	FOX, BOX, SOCKS
/y/ (as in 'yellow')	GUY, PIE, FLY
/z/ (as in 'zebra')	BEE, SEE, TREE

PATTERNED LANGUAGE

PATTERNED LANGUAGE

Patterned language in early years books refers to the repetition of words, phrases, or structures that create a predictable rhythm or sequence throughout the story.

This repetition helps young children anticipate what comes next, making the story easier to understand and engage with.

For example, in the book 'Brown Bear, Brown Bear, What Do You See?' by Bill Martin Jr. and Eric Carle, the patterned language follows a predictable sequence where each page introduces a new animal and repeats the question "What do you see?" and the response "I see a [colour] [animal] looking at me."

This repetitive structure helps children anticipate the next page and participate in the storytelling process.

Think about using patterned language where, on purpose, your story words become predictable.

This helps with engagement.

We used 'Rat -a- tat- tat - what is that?' in our book 'Katie and the Kite' and repeat it a few times.

Children love to get the hang of something - it's a great way to do with patterned language.

Try to include a pattern in your dialogue so that it sounds appealing and it flows.

PATTERNED LANGUAGE

Here are some ideas:

SEQUENTIAL ACTIONS	Create a story where the actions of the characters follow a repetitive sequence. For example, "First, the bunny hopped. Then, the bunny skipped. Finally, the bunny jumped." (rule of 3)
QUESTION AND ANSWER	Structure the story around a series of questions and answers that repeat throughout the book. For instance, "Who is hiding behind the tree? It's the squirrel with a nut!"
OPPOSITES OR CONTRASTS	Use contrasting words or phrases to create a pattern. For example, "Up, up, up the hill we climb. Down, down, down we slide."
RHYMING COUPLETS	Write in rhyming couplets where each pair of lines follows the same rhyme scheme. This can create a rhythmic pattern that children enjoy. For example, "In the forest, dark and deep, the little fox went fast asleep."
COUNTING OR ENUMERATION	Create a pattern by counting or enumerating items in the story. For instance, "One by one, the stars appeared in the sky. Two by two, the rabbits hopped by."
REFRAINS OR CHORUSES	Introduce a repeated refrain or chorus that occurs at certain intervals throughout the story. This can serve as a familiar anchor for young readers. For example, "On a cold winter's night, the snowflakes dance and twirl. Round and round they go, in a winter wonderland swirl."

PATTERNED LANGUAGE

Here are some examples of sequential actions in a story:

THE ADVENTURES OF SAMMY THE SNAIL

First, Sammy crawled slowly along the leaf.

Then, he stopped to nibble on a tasty green snack.

Finally, he slid down the stem and landed softly on the ground.

A DAY AT THE BEACH

First, Sarah built a sandcastle with her bucket and spade.

Then, she splashed in the waves and chased seagulls along the shore.

Finally, she relaxed under the shade of a palm tree with a refreshing drink.

THE BUSY BEE

First, the bee buzzed around the garden, collecting nectar from colourful flowers.

Then, she returned to her hive and danced to communicate the location of the best flowers to her fellow bees.

Finally, she capped the honey-filled comb cells with beeswax, ready for the winter months ahead.

RHYME

RHYME

You don't have to rhyme.

Don't force it or you may stray from the actual story and lose your reader.

Rhyme isn't easy for everybody - the story is more important.

Think of several ways of saying something and see which line-ending rhyme feels the best.

Read it aloud to see how well it flows.

FORMULA FOR RHYME

A basic rhyming formula for a children's story typically follows a simple AABB pattern. Here's what it looks like:

AABB Pattern:

The cat sat on the mat, (A)
He looked around, where was the rat? (A)
He saw it hiding behind the tree, (B)
And thought, "Oh dear, it's trying to flee!" (B)

WHY YOU SHOULD AVOID RHYMING IN YOUR STORY

- Crafting meaningful rhymes can be challenging.
- Forced rhymes disrupt the story's flow.
- More creativity and vocabulary use are possible without rhymes.
- Rhymes may distract readers from the story.
- Avoiding rhymes offers a refreshing change.
- Ensures accessibility across diverse audiences.

RHYME

HOUSE

| MOUSE | LOUSE | BLOUSE | SPOUSE |

TRAIN

| RAIN | PLAIN | LANE | CRANE |

MOON

| SPOON | TUNE | BALLOON | NOON |

COW

| BOW | WOW | HOW | NOW |

CHAIR

| BEAR | STARE | HAIR | DARE |

STAR

| CAR | JAR | BAR | FAR |

DOOR

| FLOOR | BORE | CHORE | SNORE |

RHYME

PHONE

CONE — ZONE — TONE — ALONE

CLOCK

ROCK — BLOCK — DOCK — FLOCK

CUP

PUP — SUP — UP — HICCUP

TREE

BEE — KNEE — FREE — SEE

FOX

BOX — SOCKS — ROCKS — BLOCKS

BOOK

LOOK — TOOK — NOOK — HOOK

BIRD

NERD — WORD — THIRD — HEARD

YOUR TURN

Decide if you want to rhyme or not, then look at your story and make a list of relevant/fun words you can rhyme with.

SECRETS TO PAGE TURNERS

SECRETS TO PAGE TURNERS

WHY DO WE WANT TO CREATE PAGE-TURNERS?

We create page-turners for children's stories to keep them engaged and excited about reading.

Page-turners captivate young readers' attention, encouraging them to continue exploring the story and fostering a love for reading from an early age.

HOW DO WE CREATE PAGE-TURNERS?

QUESTIONS	You could end it with a cliffhanger: 'What will the rabbit do?' This encourages interaction and a 'wonder' that has to be known by turning the page. This promotes thinking and discussion.
GET THEM HOOKED EARLY	Introduce your main character on the first page so the readers know who to focus on. Start in the thick of the action.
START WITH ACTION	Start with action – not backstory, drip the backstory in gradually. In 'Katie and the Kite,' we started with 'the noise' first: Rat-tat-tat-tat. Rat-tat-tat-tat. "What is that?" This provokes wonder and intrigue: 'what is it?'
START WITH A SCREAM!	Start with a scream, or other sound. Make the reader 'stop' before the story starts. Don't let them get comfortable or they will switch off. Children have a million other things they can do; play with toys, or watch TV etc. You are competing for their time and attention.

SECRETS TO PAGE TURNERS

VARY THE WORD AND SENTENCE LENGTH -

USE MINIMAL TEXT WHEN SOMETHING IS DRAMATIC

Vary the word lengths, and sentence length to make it more exciting to read.

Have a long sentence followed by a short sentence - but not all the time (or THAT would become predictable).

For example:

<u>Long sentence:</u>

The sun shone through the trees, making spots of light on the ground. Sammy the squirral ran over logs and under branches, his whiskers moving as he looked around for fun.

<u>Short sentence:</u>

Sammy heard a low growl nearby.

ADD IN PLOT TWISTS

Add them right where we are not expecting it.

When thinking of plot twists, think of where you are in your story.

Your plot twist can be something 'good' eg: something/someone who rescues your main character just at the right time, or finding something (such as treasure, food etc). Or it could be something 'bad' (the worst thing to happen, fear coming true, at the worst time).

Pick which one would be most engaging for YOUR story.

SECRETS TO PAGE TURNERS

EXAMPLES OF HOW YOU CAN MAKE YOUR CHILDREN'S BOOK A PAGE TURNER

SIMPLE LANGUAGE	The sun shines. Sammy runs.
VIVID IMAGERY	The sun glows bright. Flowers bloom.
SHORT SENTENCES	Sammy jumps. Up, up, up!
REPETITION AND PREDICTABILITY	Sammy jumps high. Again, again, again!
ENGAGING CHARACTERS	Sammy the squirrel giggles.
INTERACTIVE ELEMENTS	Can you jump like Sammy?
EXCITING PLOT TWISTS	Sammy finds a treasure hidden in the tree!
POSITIVE THEMES	Sammy shares his acorns with his friends.
ENGAGING ILLUSTRATIONS	Colourful pictures of Sammy exploring the forest.
SATISFYING RESOLUTION	Sammy and his friends have a picnic under the shining sun.

SHOW, NOT TELL

SHOW, NOT TELL

"Show, not tell" is a principle in storytelling that encourages writers to convey information and evoke emotions through actions, descriptions, and dialogue rather than simply stating them outright.

In children's stories, this technique is particularly important as it allows young readers to engage more actively with the narrative and use their imagination to visualise the events.

The purpose of "show, not tell" in children's stories is to stimulate their senses, ignite their creativity, and immerse them in the story world.

For example:

Instead of saying, "Samantha was very scared," a children's author might write:

"Samantha's heart raced as she tiptoed through the dark hallway, her hands trembling as she clutched her teddy bear tightly."

Instead of saying, "The playground was fun," an author might write:

"As Emily dashed onto the playground, she felt the springy rubber beneath her feet, the swings swaying gently in the breeze, and the laughter of her friends echoing in the air. She was bubbling with excitement about the adventures to come."

SHOW, NOT TELL

How does this look in children's stories?

AGE GROUP	For preschoolers, "show" by describing simple actions like a character playing with toys rather than "telling" their emotions directly.
CONTEXT	In a story about friendship, "show" how characters support each other through actions like sharing toys, rather than simply stating they are good friends.
EMOTIONS	Instead of saying a character is sad, "show" their sadness through actions like drooping shoulders and watery eyes.
VIVID LANGUAGE	Describe a sunny day at the beach with colourful umbrellas, crashing waves, and warm sand to "show" the setting rather than just mentioning it's a nice day.
CHARACTER DEVELOPMENT	"Show" a character's bravery by having them confront their fears, such as climbing a tree despite being scared of heights, rather than explicitly stating they are brave.

WHAT HAPPENS IF YOU DON'T SHOW AND ONLY TELL?

If you only "tell" in a children's story and don't "show," the storytelling becomes less engaging.

Children may struggle to connect with the characters and the story's events because they aren't actively experiencing them through vivid descriptions and actions.

Without showing, the story lacks excitement and may fail to capture children's imaginations, leading to a less immersive reading experience.

You want your readers to be IN the story not reading the story.

SHOW, NOT TELL
HOW TO DO IT

WHAT	HOW	EXAMPLE: 'THE THREE LITTLE PIGS'
IDENTIFY EMOTIONS	Decide which emotions you want to convey in the story.	Decide to convey fear in the story.
CHOOSE ACTIONS	Think of actions that show these emotions naturally.	The actions that show fear could include the pigs trembling, looking over their shoulders, and their hearts racing as they build their houses to protect themselves from the Big Bad Wolf.
USE DESCRIPTIVE LANGUAGE	Describe characters' movements, expressions, and surroundings vividly.	"The pigs' hooves trembled as they stacked the bricks, their ears twitching at every rustle of leaves in the wind. Dark clouds loomed overhead, casting shadows across the forest."
SHOW THROUGH DIALOGUE	Use dialogue to reveal emotions indirectly.	"I-I'm scared," stammered the youngest pig, his voice trembling. "Don't worry," replied the older pigs, "we'll be safe in our sturdy houses."
CREATE ENGAGING SCENES	Develop scenes with sensory details and character interactions.	Develop a scene where the pigs are working frantically to build their houses while the wolf lurks nearby, the tension building as they try to outsmart him.
SHOW CHARACTER GROWTH	Use actions to demonstrate how characters change throughout the story.	As the story progresses, the pigs learn the importance of hard work and perseverance. They initially build houses of straw and sticks but eventually realise the value of solid construction when the wolf blows down the weaker houses.
REVISE AND REFINE	Review the story to ensure emotions are shown, not told.	Ensure that fear is consistently shown throughout the story through actions, dialogue, and descriptive language, rather than simply telling the reader that the pigs are scared.

SHOW, NOT TELL

Here are some examples of how that can be done in stories:

SURPRISE	Tommy's eyes popped wide open and his mouth formed a big "O" shape when he tore the wrapping paper off his birthday present and found his favourite toy inside. He jumped up and down with excitement!
	Lily jumped back and let out a gasp when a colourful butterfly landed on her hand out of nowhere, her eyes shining with wonder and surprise.
	Gasping loudly and jumping back with wide eyes when something unexpected happens.
	Dropping a book or toy in shock and staring with mouth hanging open.
	Covering mouth with hands and eyes widening in disbelief.
	Clutching onto a friend or family member tightly when startled.
	Letting out a squeal of surprise and then laughing nervously afterward.

SHOW, NOT TELL

Here are some examples of how that can be done in stories:

DISGUST	Emily wrinkled her nose and pushed her plate away when she spotted a slimy green vegetable mixed in with her mashed potatoes, making a face like she tasted something really yucky!
	Timmy's face scrunched up in disgust as he carefully picked up a stinky sock from the floor, holding it away from his nose and quickly throwing it in the laundry basket.
	Making exaggerated gagging noises and sticking out tongue at something gross.
	Scrunching up nose and squinting eyes at an unpleasant smell.
	Wiping hands on clothes and shaking them as if trying to get rid of something dirty.
	Pushing food away with a disgusted expression and shuddering.
	Scrubbing hands vigorously with soap and water after touching something yucky.

SHOW, NOT TELL

Here are some examples of how that can be done in stories:

FRUSTRATION	Sarah slammed her hands on the table and let out a frustrated groan when she couldn't fit the puzzle pieces together, tossing them aside and crossing her arms with a huff.
	Ethan kicked his crayons off the table and stomped his feet when he couldn't draw a perfect circle, crumpling up his paper and throwing it in the trash, feeling really angry and upset.
	Pounding fists on the table and furrowing eyebrows in frustration.
	Biting lip and pulling at hair in annoyance.
	Letting out a loud sigh and rolling eyes dramatically.
	Stomping feet and muttering angrily under breath.
	Crumpling up paper and throwing it across the room in frustration.

SHOW, NOT TELL

Here are some examples of how that can be done in stories:

ANXIETY	Jake tapped his foot nervously and bit his lip as he looked around the room before his big presentation, his heart pounding fast and his stomach feeling queasy with nerves.
	Mia chewed on her fingernails and twisted her hair around her finger as she waited to start at a new school, feeling jittery and scared about making new friends.
	Fidgeting with hands or objects and tapping foot nervously.
	Gnawing on fingernails and avoiding eye contact.
	Pacing back and forth with a worried expression.
	Breathing quickly and shallowly, feeling clammy hands and a tight chest.
	Stuttering or stumbling over words when speaking due to nervousness.

SHOW, NOT TELL

Here are some examples of how that can be done in stories:

JEALOUSY

Lily clenched her fists and glared at her friend playing with the new toy, wishing it was hers and feeling a tight knot in her stomach.

Tommy's face turned red and he crossed his arms as he watched his sister get praised for her drawing, feeling a pang of jealousy and sadness inside.

Crossing arms tightly over chest and glaring at someone else's belongings or achievements.

Letting out an envious sigh and looking away when others receive praise or attention.

Making snide comments or rolling eyes when someone else gets what they want.

Sulking in a corner and refusing to join in activities when feeling left out.

Clenching fists and grinding teeth when seeing others succeed.

SHOW, NOT TELL

Here are some examples of how that can be done in stories:

CURIOSITY	Emily tiptoed closer to the mysterious box in the attic, her heart thumping loudly in her chest as she reached out to lift the lid and uncover its secrets, feeling excited and curious.
	Timmy crouched down low and peered into the bushes, his eyes wide with curiosity as he tried to figure out what was making the strange noise, feeling a mix of nervousness and excitement.
	Leaning forward with wide eyes and asking lots of questions about something new or mysterious.
	Investigating with hands and eyes, turning objects over and examining them closely.
	Squatting down to peer at something from different angles, trying to uncover hidden details.
	Following a strange sound or smell to its source, eager to discover its origin.

SHOW, NOT TELL

Here are some examples of how that can be done in stories:

LOVE	Sarah wrapped her arms around her puppy and squeezed tight, planting kisses on its head and feeling a warm, fuzzy feeling in her heart.
	Ethan gave his mom a big hug and handed her a homemade card, smiling from ear to ear and feeling really happy and loved.
	Smiling softly and reaching out for a hug or cuddle.
	Offering a handmade gift or drawing with a big grin.
	Sharing a secret or whispering affectionate words to a loved one.
	Offering a comforting touch or holding hands tightly.
	Spending quality time together, laughing and enjoying each other's company.

SHOW, NOT TELL

Here are some examples of how that can be done in stories:

CONFUSION	Jake scratched his head and furrowed his brow as he stared at the maths problem, feeling puzzled and unsure of what to do next.
	Mia frowned and bit her lip as she read the complicated directions, feeling confused and frustrated about where to start.
	Scratching head while staring blankly at a confusing problem.
	Tapping pencil on chin and tilting head to the side in puzzlement.
	Asking for clarification multiple times with a confused expression.
	Rubbing eyes and shaking head as if trying to clear foggy thoughts.

SHOW, NOT TELL

Here are some examples of how that can be done in stories:

LONELINESS	Lily sat down on the swing by herself and hugged her knees, watching other kids play and feeling a lump in her throat, wishing she had someone to play with.
	Tommy hugged his stuffed bear tightly and looked at the family photo on his nightstand, feeling tears prick at the corners of his eyes as he missed his parents, feeling really alone.
	Hugging oneself tightly and looking around with a sad expression.
	Sitting apart from others with shoulders hunched and head down.
	Staring out of a window or into the distance with a distant look in eyes.
	Drawing or writing in a journal as a way to express feelings of isolation.

SHOW, NOT TELL

Here are some examples of how that can be done in stories:

CONTENTMENT	Emily snuggled under the soft blankets and let out a happy sigh, closing her eyes and feeling warm and cosy.
	Timmy skipped through the park, feeling the warm sun on his face and listening to the birds chirping, feeling peaceful and content.
	Letting out a relaxed sigh and leaning back with a peaceful expression.
	Curling up with a favourite book or toy and smiling contentedly.
	Taking deep breaths and savouring the moment with closed eyes.
	Humming a happy tune or softly singing to oneself.
	Wrapping oneself in a warm blanket and snuggling into a comfortable position

YOUR TURN

Pick 3 different emotions you want to convey and write different scenes that are related to your story to SHOW these emotions.

Write 1-2 scenes from your story first.
Then, pick sections where you can SHOW and not just TELL what is happening.

WRITING YOUR STORY

PUTTING IT ALL TOGETHER

Title: ....

Genre: ....

Theme: ....

Emotion/s I want to include: ....

Settings: ....

My main character is: ....

Do I have a villain? If so, who or what?: ....

Do I have a helper/ally? If so who or what?: ....

What is my main character's overall goal?: ....

What is the overall obstacle?: ....

What is the main focus of my story? (Educate, entertain or both): ....

What exactly is my focus? (numbers, shapes, letters, sounds, days of the week, important messages etc.): ....

My story is about: (Write a short sentence): ....

What are the most common images that appear in my story? (Eg: objects that are circle shaped, numbers, football, clowns, dragon etc.): ....

STRUCTURE

Write out your story structure in more detail.

But NOW include an illustration or two you could use in your picture book that depicts that scene. Eg. if your character plays football the image could be a football, a park etc,

Add dialogue and basic descriptions.

ELEMENT	IDEA	ILLUSTRATION I COULD INCLUDE?
INTRODUCTION TO MAIN CHARACTER		
INTRODUCE PROBLEM		
INCITING EVENT (WHAT DOES THE MAIN CHARACTER NEED TO DO AND WHY)		
THEIR OVERALL GOAL		
STEP 1 TO ACHIEVE THAT GOAL		
OBSTACLE TO THAT		
CONSEQUENCE		

STRUCTURE

ELEMENT	IDEA	ILLUSTRATION I COULD INCLUDE?
STEP 2 TO ACHIEVE THAT GOAL		
OBSTACLE TO THAT		
CONSEQUENCE		
PLOT TWIST		
STEP 3 TO ACHIEVE THAT GOAL		
OBSTACLE TO THAT		
CONSEQUENCE		
ENDING/RESOLUTION		

YOUR TURN

Write your story scene by scene IN MORE DETAIL - INCLUDE DIALOGUE AND DESCRIPTIONS.

For each scene, think of 1-2 images that would showcase that scene.

SCENE 1 INTRODUCE CHARACTER	
SCENE 2	
SCENE 3	
SCENE 4	
SCENE 5	
SCENE 6	

YOUR TURN

Write your story scene by scene IN MORE DETAIL - INCLUDE DIALOGUE AND DESCRIPTIONS.

For each scene, think of 1-2 images that would showcase that scene.

SCENE 7

SCENE 8

SCENE 9

SCENE 10

SCENE 11

SCENE 12
ENDING

EDITING YOUR STORY

EDITING YOUR STORY

Editing is vital.

Clarity and understanding: Children have developing language skills, so clear and simple language helps them understand the story better.

Engagement: Age-appropriate language keeps children engaged and interested in the story, preventing confusion or boredom.

Safety and sensitivity: Children's stories should avoid language or themes that could be inappropriate, offensive, or harmful to young readers.

Learning and development: Well-edited stories with the appropriate language can support children's language development and literacy skills.

Don't be scared to get feedback on your story from an editor, beta readers or people you can trust to give you constructive criticism.

The last people you want to test it out on is your reader - that's too late!

Bad reviews and reputation are at stake here!

HOW TO EDIT YOUR STORY

Less is more!

Avoid unnecessary long sentences.

Use 5 words instead of 10 – get there quicker.

Don't lead with your ego – your story (and your reader) come first!

HOW WE DO IT

Do another read-over after you have had a break.

Read it aloud to see how it flows and correct any mistakes.

Run it through software such as Grammarly to check typos etc.

Run it through software called Hemmingway to see which 'grade' your story is pitched at. The lower the better for children – aim for grades 1-2.

PART 3

CREATING YOUR STORY BOOK

CREATING YOUR BOOK

You've written your story. Now you need to create your book, right?

Illustrations happen after the writing is done. You can get illustrations done a variety of ways:

- You can do it yourself.
- You can outsource it - this can cost £500-£3000+ per book due to skill.

For our children's books, we use a software programme called Canva.

There is a free version of Canva but it has limited capabilities.

If you're serious about designing your own children's book, we recommend you invest in the Pro version of Canva. It is WELL worth the money!

Other software you can use to create your book:

Adobe Illustrator	Professional vector graphics editor for detailed illustrations.
Procreate	iPad app for hand-drawn illustrations with various brushes.
Affinity Designer	Powerful vector graphics editor similar to Illustrator.
Clip Studio Paint	Versatile digital art software for dynamic illustrations.
CorelDRAW	User-friendly vector graphics editor for layouts and illustrations.
Inkscape	Free and open-source alternative to Illustrator.
Krita	Free painting program with customisable brushes.
MediBang Paint	Free software for digital painting and comic creation.
Pixlr	Online photo editor for enhancing illustrations and layouts.

CREATING YOUR BOOK

Things to consider:

- Match the colours and vibe to the story - bright colours work best.

If your story is set in space, look on Amazon. Check out the bestsellers and look at their front covers, fonts and illustrations. This can be good inspiration.

DO NOT COPY THEM.

- Start with reading each page - think of initial sketches and ideas for action.

<u>For example</u>: 'In a sunny garden, Lily laughed as she chased a colourful butterfly. The butterfly danced around her, making Lily giggle with delight.'

Some ideas for illustrations/graphics for that page could be the main character, a colourful butterfly, or both (depending on illustration capabilities).

<u>Another example:</u>

'In a galaxy far away, Captain Max and Robo zoomed through space in their Space Rocket. They spotted a comet and chased after it, eager for adventure.'

Ideas for pictures - space rocket, comet - or both!

FRONT COVERS

FRONT COVERS

The front cover of a children's storybook plays a crucial role in capturing the attention of young readers and enticing them to pick up the book. Here's why:

Creates a positive first impression: It's the first thing children see, so an engaging cover sparks their curiosity about the story.

Attracts attention: Colourful designs stand out on shelves, drawing children in with captivating imagery.

Reflects the story: The cover gives a glimpse into the story's world and characters, enticing children to explore further.

Builds brand recognition: Consistent cover designs help children easily recognise and connect with their favourite authors or series.

WHAT YOU SHOULD INCLUDE

- Bright colours
- The main character on the front
- No more than 3 words for a title
- Big font for the title

FRONT COVERS

WHAT EXACTLY TO INCLUDE ON THE FRONT COVER

Title: The title of the book is prominently displayed to clearly indicate what the story is about.

Author and illustrator: The names of the author and illustrator (if different) are usually featured on the front cover to give credit for their contributions to the book.

Illustrations: Eye-catching illustrations or images related to the story are often included to visually represent the characters, setting, or theme of the book.

Key characters or scenes: The front cover may feature key characters or scenes from the story to give readers a glimpse into the book's content and entice them to explore further.

Design elements: Various design elements such as colour schemes, typography, and layout are used to create a visually appealing and cohesive cover design that reflects the tone and style of the book.

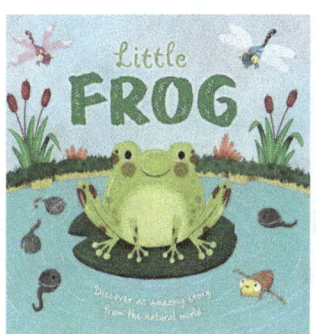  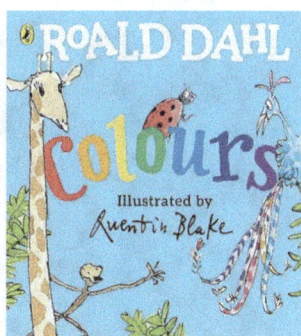 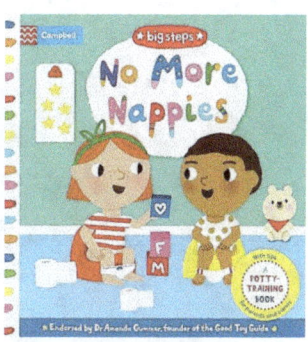

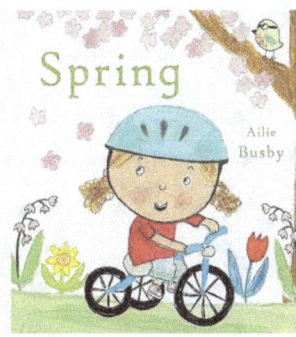  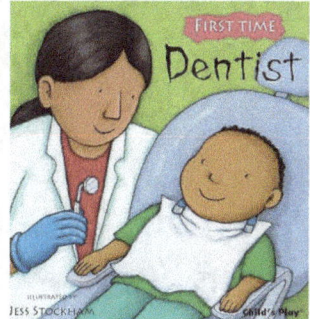 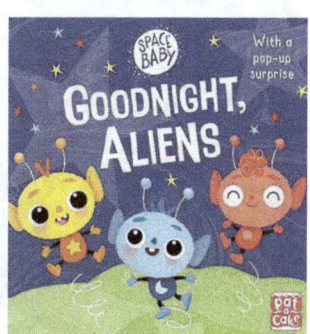

LAYOUT

LAYOUT

Children's books are designed using a layout format called 'spreads.' These are double pages and generally feature a main background image layered with images and text which tell the story.

There are usually 12 spreads, giving the book 26 pages when you include the first and last page.

Here is an example of how your template will look:

FIRST PAGE

LAST PAGE

PUBLISHING

PUBLISHING

You can self-publish or go traditionally published.

Self-published literally means that you do everything. This includes writing, editing, sorting the front cover, publishing on platforms such as Amazon etc., and doing the marketing.

Traditionally published means you submit your story idea to a publisher and they take care of everything and you get a split of the royalties (money from sales).

For self-publishing, you take ALL the royalties, but you have to pay for everything.

No publisher will EVER ask an author to contribute financially upfront or at any time.

This would be a scam.

Get submission details from books such as: Children's Writers and Artists Yearbook

Self-publishing:

- You will need an 'Amazon Kindle Direct Publishing' account
- Fill in all details.
- Create your book (via graphic designers or you do it yourself using Canva etc)
- Upload to Amazon - include title, book description etc.
- Wait for it to be approved.
- It goes live
- Promote!

YOUR CHECKLIST

YOUR CHECKLIST

HAVE YOU DONE THE FOLLOWING?	✓
GONE ONTO AMAZON TO HAVE A LOOK AT THE BESTSELLERS?	
PICKED YOUR GENRE	
HAD A LOOK AT THE BESTSELLERS IN YOUR GENRE TO SEE THE COMMONALITIES?	
CREATED A CATCHY TITLE?	
CREATED A MEMORABLE CHARACTER?	
CREATED A VILLAIN OF SOME KIND (HUMAN OR NOT)?	
GIVEN YOUR CHARACTER A COMPELLING GOAL?	
COME UP WITH THREE OBSTACLES TO THAT GOAL?	
COME UP WITH CONSEQUENCES FOR EACH OBSTACLE?	
CREATED A PLOT TWIST?	

YOUR CHECKLIST

HAVE YOU DONE THE FOLLOWING?

STARTED WITH ACTION?

CREATED A CAPTIVATING ENDING THAT IS THE PERFECT (AND UNPREDICTABLE RESOLUTION)

INCLUDED A THEME/MESSAGE?

USED ANY OF THE FOLLOWING: PATTERNED LANGUAGE, ONOMATOPOEIA, ALLITERATION ETC...?

KEPT THE TEXT 1-2 SYLLABLES (3 ON SOME OCCASIONS)?

INCLUDED SOME CLIFF-HANGERS AT THE BOTTOM OF SOME OF THE PAGES?

KEPT THE WORD COUNT TO UNDER 1000 WORDS?

DESIGNED AN EYE-CATCHING FRONT COVER?

RESOURCE TOOLKIT

COMMONALITIES WITH THE BESTSELLERS

ENGAGING CHARACTERS — Many bestsellers feature memorable and relatable characters that children can connect with emotionally. These characters often have unique personalities, quirks, and traits that make them appealing to young readers.

VIBRANT ILLUSTRATIONS — Eye-catching and vibrant illustrations play a crucial role in children's picture books. Bestsellers often feature illustrations that are colourful, detailed, and visually appealing, capturing the attention of young readers and enhancing the storytelling experience.

SIMPLE AND CLEAR STORYLINES — Successful children's picture books typically have simple and easy-to-follow storylines that are appropriate for the target age group. These stories often straightforwardly convey important messages or themes, making them accessible to young readers.

POSITIVE THEMES — Many bestsellers focus on positive themes such as friendship, kindness, courage, and perseverance. These themes resonate with children and help instil important values and lessons in an engaging and relatable way.

INTERACTIVE ELEMENTS — Some bestsellers incorporate interactive elements such as lift-the-flap pages, touch-and-feel textures, or hidden surprises that encourage active participation and engagement from young readers.

HUMOUR AND PLAYFULNESS — Humorous and playful elements can make children's picture books highly enjoyable for both children and adults. Many bestsellers feature whimsical humour, clever wordplay, or funny situations that elicit laughter and keep readers entertained.

EMPOWERING MESSAGES — Top-selling children's picture books often include empowering messages that promote self-confidence, resilience, and inclusivity. These messages empower children to embrace their individuality, overcome challenges, and make a positive difference in the world around them.

APPEALING COVERS — The cover of a children's picture book is often the first thing that catches a reader's eye. Bestsellers typically have visually appealing covers that feature captivating artwork, intriguing characters, and vibrant colours, enticing readers to pick up the book and explore its contents.

GENRE DEFINITIONS

ABC AND COUNTING BOOKS	Books that teach the alphabet, numbers, or basic counting concepts through engaging stories or rhymes.
ADVENTURE STORIES	Exciting tales that take young readers on journeys filled with action, exploration, and discovery.
ANIMAL STORIES	Stories featuring animals as main characters, often with anthropomorphic traits, conveying valuable lessons or morals.
BEDTIME STORIES	Books with calming narratives and soothing illustrations, perfect for winding down before bedtime.
FAIRY TALES AND FOLK TALES	Classic stories passed down through generations, featuring magical elements, moral lessons, and familiar characters.
FRIENDSHIP STORIES	Tales focusing on friendship, teaching children valuable lessons about cooperation, empathy, and kindness.
HUMOROUS STORIES	Books aiming to entertain children through funny situations, quirky characters, and playful language.
INTERACTIVE BOOKS	Books encouraging participation through lift-the-flap, touch-and-feel, or other interactive elements.
LEARNING CONCEPTS	Books introducing and reinforcing basic concepts like colours, shapes, sizes, opposites, and emotions through engaging narratives.
PICTURE BOOKS	Heavily illustrated with minimal text, perfect for young children to engage with the story through visuals.
SEASONAL AND HOLIDAY BOOKS	Stories revolving around specific seasons, holidays, or celebrations, helping children understand and appreciate cultural traditions.

GENRE TOOLKIT

	FANTASY
COLOURS ON BOOK COVERS	Bold, vibrant colours such as deep blues, rich greens, and shimmering golds.
FAMOUS STORIES	'Harry Potter' series by J.K. Rowling, 'The Hobbit' by J.R.R. Tolkien
MOST COMMON STORYLINE	Heroes embarking on epic quests to defeat dark forces or restore balance to magical realms.
MOST COMMON MAIN CHARACTER	The chosen one or an unlikely hero with magical abilities or a special destiny.
MOST COMMON VILLAIN	Dark wizards, evil sorcerers, or powerful mythical creatures threatening the world.
MOST COMMON THEME	Good vs. evil, the power of friendship, and the importance of bravery.
MOST COMMON SETTINGS	Enchanted forests, medieval kingdoms, mystical castles, and otherworldly realms.

GENRE TOOLKIT

	ADVENTURE
COLOURS ON BOOK COVERS	Dynamic colours like bright reds, vibrant oranges, and adventurous blues.
FAMOUS STORIES	'The Adventures of Tintin' series by Hergé, 'Treasure Island' by Robert Louis Stevenson.
MOST COMMON STORYLINE	Courageous characters embarking on daring journeys to discover hidden treasures or save the day.
MOST COMMON MAIN CHARACTER	Fearless explorers or young protagonists eager for adventure.
MOST COMMON VILLAIN	Pirates, villains seeking treasure, or natural forces like storms and wild animals.
MOST COMMON THEME	Courage, friendship, and the thrill of exploration.
MOST COMMON SETTINGS	Mysterious islands, ancient ruins, dense jungles, and uncharted territories.

GENRE TOOLKIT

FAIRYTALES

COLOURS ON BOOK COVERS	Soft pastels such as light pinks, gentle blues, and dreamy yellows.
FAMOUS STORIES	'Cinderella' by Charles Perrault, 'Snow White' by Brothers Grimm.
MOST COMMON STORYLINE	Royalty overcoming adversity with the help of magical assistance or true love's kiss.
MOST COMMON MAIN CHARACTER	Princes, princesses, and humble protagonists facing trials and tribulations.
MOST COMMON VILLAIN	Wicked stepmothers, evil witches, or enchantresses casting curses.
MOST COMMON THEME	Good triumphing over evil, the importance of kindness, and the rewards of perseverance.
MOST COMMON SETTINGS	Medieval villages, enchanted forests, grand castles, and magical kingdoms.

GENRE TOOLKIT

MYSTERY

COLOURS ON BOOK COVERS	Dark and mysterious colours like deep purples, ominous blacks, and shadowy greys.
FAMOUS STORIES	'Nancy Drew' series by Carolyn Keene, 'The Hardy Boys' series by Franklin W. Dixon.
MOST COMMON STORYLINE	Young detectives solving perplexing puzzles and unravelling secrets to uncover the truth.
MOST COMMON MAIN CHARACTER	Clever sleuths or curious children with a knack for solving mysteries.
MOST COMMON VILLAIN	Crafty criminals, sneaky thieves, or elusive culprits hiding their true identities.
MOST COMMON THEME	Problem-solving, justice prevailing, and the thrill of discovery.
MOST COMMON SETTINGS	Spooky mansions, quaint villages, mysterious islands, and bustling cities.

GENRE TOOLKIT

ANIMAL STORIES

COLOURS ON BOOK COVERS	Playful and vibrant colours like cheerful yellows, bright greens, and earthy browns.
FAMOUS STORIES	'Charlotte's Web' by E.B. White, 'Watership Down' by Richard Adams.
MOST COMMON STORYLINE	Anthropomorphic animals embarking on adventures, facing challenges, and learning valuable lessons.
MOST COMMON MAIN CHARACTER	Animals with human-like qualities, such as intelligence, emotions, and friendships.
MOST COMMON VILLAIN	Predators threatening the safety or harmony of the animal community.
MOST COMMON THEME	Friendship, bravery, and the interconnectedness of all living beings.
MOST COMMON SETTINGS	Forests, meadows, farms, and other natural habitats.

GENRE TOOLKIT

SCIENCE FICTION

COLOURS ON BOOK COVERS	Futuristic colours like metallic silver, neon greens, and electric blues.
FAMOUS STORIES	'A Wrinkle in Time' by Madeleine L'Engle, 'The Giver' by Lois Lowry.
MOST COMMON STORYLINE	Characters navigating futuristic societies, encountering advanced technology, and exploring the cosmos.
MOST COMMON MAIN CHARACTER	Adventurous youths or intrepid explorers thrust into extraordinary circumstances.
MOST COMMON VILLAIN	Oppressive governments, malevolent aliens, or rogue AIs threatening humanity's existence.
MOST COMMON THEME	Exploration, the impact of technology on society, and the quest for knowledge.
MOST COMMON SETTINGS	Dystopian cities, space stations, alien planets, and futuristic landscapes.

GENRE TOOLKIT

HUMOUR

COLOURS ON BOOK COVERS	Bright and whimsical colours like cheerful yellows, playful oranges, and vibrant greens.
FAMOUS STORIES	'Diary of a Wimpy Kid' series by Jeff Kinney, 'Captain Underpants' series by Dav Pilkey.
MOST COMMON STORYLINE	Hilarious misadventures and absurd situations that leave readers laughing out loud.
MOST COMMON MAIN CHARACTER	Eccentric or mischievous protagonists with a knack for getting into comical predicaments.
MOST COMMON VILLAIN	Antagonists who serve as foils to the protagonist's antics, often with exaggerated traits.
MOST COMMON THEME	The power of laughter, friendship, and the joy of embracing one's uniqueness.
MOST COMMON SETTINGS	Ordinary neighbourhoods, wacky schools, and quirky towns filled with colourful characters.

GENRE TOOLKIT

PICTURE BOOKS

COLOURS ON BOOK COVERS	Bright and playful colours that catch the eye and evoke a sense of joy and wonder.
FAMOUS STORIES	'The Very Hungry Caterpillar' by Eric Carle, 'Goodnight Moon' by Margaret Wise Brown.
MOST COMMON STORYLINE	Simple and heart-warming narratives with universal themes that resonate with young readers.
MOST COMMON MAIN CHARACTER	Adorable animals, imaginative children, or endearing creatures experiencing everyday adventures.
MOST COMMON VILLAIN	In picture books, conflict is often minimal or resolved through gentle means, with no clear villain.
MOST COMMON THEME	Friendship, imagination, bedtime routines, and the beauty of nature.
MOST COMMON SETTINGS	Cosy homes, bustling streets, fantastical worlds, and serene natural landscapes.

MOST COMMON EMOTIONS

HAPPY	SAD	ANGRY
EXCITED	SCARED	SURPRISED
CONFUSED	PROUD	SHY
CALM	SILLY	GRUMPY
CURIOUS	LONELY	NERVOUS
EMBARRASSED	LOVING	CONTENT
FRUSTRATED	BRAVE	LOYAL

MOST COMMON CHARACTERS

ANIMALS	CHILDREN	FANTASTICAL CREATURES
FAIRYTALE CHARACTERS	EVERYDAY OBJECTS OR TOYS	MAGICAL BEINGS
PARENTAL FIGURES	EXPLORERS OR ADVENTURERS	FRIENDS
SUPERHEROES OR HEROINES	DRAGON	UNICORN
MONSTER	PRINCESS	KNIGHT

CHARACTER DESCRIPTIONS

MAGICAL UNICORN	A majestic unicorn with shimmering fur and a magical horn, who spreads joy and wonder wherever they go.
BRAVE FIREFIGHTER	A courageous firefighter who bravely battles flames and saves lives, always ready to rush to the rescue.
ENCHANTING FAIRY PRINCESS	An enchanting fairy princess who lives in a magical kingdom, using her powers to protect her realm and help those in need.
ADVENTUROUS ASTRONAUT	An adventurous astronaut who explores the cosmos, discovering new planets and encountering alien life forms.
WIZARD	A whimsical wizard with a knack for casting spells and brewing potions, embarking on quests to defeat dark forces and restore peace to the land.
GENTLE GIANT	A gentle giant who lives in the mountains, befriending woodland creatures and using their strength to protect the forest.
CLEVER CHILD DETECTIVE	A clever child detective who solves mysteries and puzzles, using their wit and keen observation skills to crack the case.
MAGICAL DRAGON	A friendly dragon with colourful scales and a playful spirit, who befriends humans and embarks on exciting adventures.
ADVENTUROUS EXPLORER	An adventurous explorer who travels to distant lands, uncovering ancient treasures and encountering exotic cultures.
SUPERHERO	An imaginative superhero with extraordinary powers, who fights villains and protects the city from harm.

CHARACTER DESCRIPTIONS

KINDHEARTED PRINCESS	A kindhearted princess who cares for her kingdom and its people, always putting others' needs before her own.
WISE ELDER	A wise elder who shares wisdom and guidance with young adventurers, drawing from their years of experience and knowledge.
CHEERFUL CLOWN	A cheerful clown who brings laughter and joy to children everywhere, with their silly antics and colourful costumes.
MYSTERIOUS MAGICIAN	A mysterious magician who performs amazing tricks and illusions, keeping audiences spellbound with their magic shows.
RESILIENT SURVIVOR	A resilient survivor who overcomes challenges and adversity, demonstrating strength and determination in the face of hardship.
ATHLETE	An enthusiastic athlete who excels in sports and competitions, inspiring others with their passion and dedication.
NATURE GUARDIAN	A nature guardian who protects the environment and its creatures, advocating for conservation and sustainability.
CREATIVE ARTIST	A creative artist who expresses themselves through painting, drawing, or sculpting, using their imagination to create beautiful works of art.
LOYAL KNIGHT	A loyal knight who serves their king and defends the realm from threats, embodying honour, courage, and chivalry.
CARING NURSE	A caring nurse who tends to the sick and injured, providing comfort and healing with their gentle touch and compassionate care.

CHARACTER DESCRIPTIONS

DARING PIRATE CAPTAIN	A daring pirate captain who sails the high seas in search of treasure, facing off against rival pirates and outwitting danger.
ADVENTUROUS MOUNTAINEER	An adventurous mountaineer who climbs the tallest peaks, overcoming obstacles and embracing the thrill of the ascent.
COURAGEOUS POLICE OFFICER	A courageous police officer who upholds the law and protects the community, serving as a beacon of safety and justice.
GENTLE SHEPHERD	A gentle shepherd who cares for their flock of sheep, guiding them through the meadows and keeping them safe from harm.
INVENTIVE ENGINEER	An inventive engineer who designs and builds amazing machines and gadgets, pushing the boundaries of innovation and technology.
CURIOUS ARCHAEOLOGIST	A curious archaeologist who explores ancient ruins and digs up artefacts, piecing together clues from the past to uncover lost civilisations.
MYSTICAL SORCERER	A mystical sorcerer who harnesses the power of magic and spells, delving into the arcane arts to unlock hidden knowledge and mysteries.
ECCENTRIC INVENTOR	An eccentric inventor who creates quirky contraptions and gadgets, using their imagination and resourcefulness to solve problems in unconventional ways.
LOVABLE ROBOT	A lovable robot with a heart of gold, who learns about friendship and emotions while navigating the world with their mechanical abilities.
WISE OWL	A wise owl who perches in the treetops, offering sage advice and guidance to travellers who seek their wisdom.

OTHER WAYS OF GENERATING IDEAS

USING OPPOSITES TO CREATE INTERESTING STORYLINES

A LION WHO CAN'T ROAR	Despite lacking a roar, the lion discovers his talent for creating beautiful music with other animals, uniting the kingdom in harmony.
A DOG WHO CAN'T BARK	This dog learns to express himself through painting, becoming a renowned artist in the animal community.
A CAT WHO'S ALLERGIC TO FUR	Despite her allergy, the cat becomes a famous fashion designer for fur coats, promoting faux fur and eco-friendly fashion.
A BIRD WHO CAN'T FLY	Determined, the bird trains tirelessly until he learns to soar, fulfilling his dream of migrating with his flock.
A FISH WHO CAN'T SWIM	Through ingenuity and determination, the fish invents a device to explore the world outside the water, inspiring others to push boundaries, but then loves the ocean.
A BEAR WHO'S AFRAID OF THE DARK	Overcoming his fear, the bear discovers the beauty of the night sky and becomes an astronomy enthusiast, teaching others about the stars.
A RABBIT WHO'S AFRAID OF CARROTS	Through a culinary adventure, the rabbit discovers a love for cooking and opens a successful restaurant featuring carrot-based dishes.

OTHER WAYS OF GENERATING IDEAS

USING OPPOSITES TO CREATE INTERESTING STORYLINES

A MOUSE WHO'S AFRAID OF CHEESE	Despite his fear, the mouse musters the courage to navigate a cheese maze to rescue his family, learning bravery in the process.
A TURTLE WHO'S AFRAID OF MOVING FAST	Slow and steady, the turtle wins a race against faster animals, proving that perseverance and determination lead to success.
A HORSE WHO'S AFRAID OF HEIGHTS	With patience and encouragement, the horse conquers his fear and excels in show jumping, inspiring others with his bravery.
A BEE WHO'S AFRAID OF FLOWERS	Overcoming her fear, the bee discovers the importance of pollination and becomes an advocate for flower preservation.
A SNAIL WHO'S AFRAID OF BEING SLOW	Despite his pace, the snail embarks on a journey around the world, showcasing the beauty of taking things one step at a time.
A FROG WHO'S AFRAID OF WATER	Through resilience, the frog overcomes his fear and saves his friends during a flood, becoming a hero in the amphibian community.
A KANGAROO WHO'S AFRAID OF JUMPING	With the support of friends, the kangaroo learns to embrace his unique talents and leads a dance troupe, showcasing his rhythmic hopping skills.

FAMILY MEMBERS

MUM/MOM/MOTHER	DAD/FATHER	BROTHER
SISTER	GRANDMA	GRANDPA
AUNT	UNCLE	COUSIN
BABY	NIECE	NEPHEW
STEP-MUM	STEP-DAD	STEP-BROTHER
STEP-SISTER	HALF-SIBLING	FOSTER PARENT
GUARDIAN	FAVOURITE PET	GREAT-GRAN

MOST COMMON ANIMALS

DOG	CAT	BIRD	CHICKEN
ELEPHANT	LION	GIRAFFE	FROG
MONKEY	TIGER	BEAR	FISH
RABBIT	HORSE	COW	BUTTERFLY
PIG	SHEEP	DUCK	SNAKE

MOST COMMON SEA CREATURES

FISH	DOLPHIN	SHARK	OCTOPUS	SEA OTTER
SEAHORSE	CRAB	JELLYFISH	TURTLE	MANATEE (SEA COW)
STARFISH	LOBSTER	SQUID	CLOWNFISH	WHALE
SWORDFISH	SEAL	PENGUIN	EEL	SEA URCHIN

MOST COMMON CREEPY CRAWLIES

ANT	BEE	BUTTERFLY	WASP	LADYBUG
GRASSHOPPER	DRAGONFLY	BEETLE	PRAYING MANTIS	CATERPILLAR
CRICKET	FIREFLY	MOSQUITO	SPIDER	MOTH

MAGICAL CREATURES

MERMAID	UNICORN	FAIRY	DRAGON	CENTAUR
TROLL	GNOME	PIXIE	ELF	LEPRECHAUN
YETI	WITCH	WIZARD	GENIE	MAGICIAN

MOST COMMON FRUITS

APPLE	BANANA	ORANGE	GRAPES
WATERMELON	PINEAPPLE	MANGO	PEAR
PEACH	PLUM	CHERRY	BLUEBERRY
BLACKBERRY	LEMON	LIME	CRANBERRY
STRAWBERRY	KIWI	RASPBERRY	BLUEBERRY

MOST COMMON VEGETABLES

CARROT	BROCCOLI	TOMATO	CUCUMBER
LETTUCE	SPINACH	PEAS	CORN
ONION	GARLIC	CAULIFLOWER	CELERY
POTATO	BELL PEPPER	GREEN BEANS	SWEET POTATO

OBJECTS THAT CAN BE CHARACTERS

ACCORDION	The Accordion could be a musical character who loves playing lively tunes and bringing joy to those who hear them.
BALLOON	The Balloon could be a cheerful and uplifting character who floats through the air, spreading happiness and laughter wherever they go.
CRAYON	The Crayon could be a colourful and creative character who brings drawings to life with their vibrant personality and artistic flair.
DOLL	The Doll could be a friendly and nurturing character who comforts children and becomes their loyal companion on imaginative adventures.
ENVELOPE	The Envelope could be a curious and adventurous character who travels far and wide, delivering messages and secrets to their recipients.
FLAG	The Flag could be a proud and patriotic character who represents their country or community, inspiring unity and pride among their fellow citizens.
GUITAR	The Guitar could be a talented musician who strums melodic tunes and serenades listeners with their soulful melodies.
HAT	The Hat could be a fashionable and stylish character who loves trying on different accessories, always staying ahead of the latest trends.
ICE CREAM CONE	The Ice Cream Cone could be a sweet and playful character who brings joy to children with their delicious treats and silly antics.
JIGSAW PUZZLE PIECE	The Jigsaw Puzzle could be a patient and cooperative character who enjoys solving puzzles and challenges, teaching children the value of teamwork and perseverance.

OBJECTS THAT CAN BE CHARACTERS

KITE	The Kite could be a free-spirited character who soars through the sky, embracing the joy of flight and inspiring children to reach new heights.
LANTERN	The Lantern could be a guiding light character who leads children through dark and mysterious places, illuminating their path with courage and hope.
MAGNIFYING GLASS	The Magnifying Glass could be a curious and investigative character who helps children solve mysteries and uncover hidden secrets, encouraging them to explore their surroundings.
NOTEBOOK	The Notebook could be a creative character who loves writing stories and drawing pictures, capturing memories and inspiring imagination.
ORIGAMI GAME	The Origami Game could be a graceful and elegant character who symbolises peace and beauty, teaching children the art of patience and precision.
PIANO	The Piano could be a talented musician character who plays classical melodies and composes their own music, enchanting audiences with their skill and passion.
QUILL	The Quill could be a poetic character who writes heartfelt letters and verses, expressing emotions and capturing moments with their eloquent words.
RAINBOW	The Rainbow could be a colourful and magical character who brings hope and joy to children with their vibrant hues and promise of better days.
SAILBOAT	The Sailboat could be an adventurous character who sets sail on the open seas, exploring distant shores and embracing the thrill of the unknown.

OBJECTS THAT CAN BE CHARACTERS

TELESCOPE	The Telescope could be an insightful character who helps children see things from a different perspective and encourages them to reach for the stars.
UMBRELLA	The Umbrella could be a protective character who shields children from rainstorms and showers them with comfort and warmth during stormy weather.
VIOLIN	The Violin could be a graceful and expressive character who plays beautiful melodies and touches hearts with their soulful music.
WAND	The Wand could be a magical character who grants wishes and casts spells, teaching children the power of imagination and belief in the impossible.
XYLOPHONE	The Xylophone could be a playful character who makes music with colourful bars and mallets, inspiring children to create their own melodies.
YO-YO	The Yo-yo could be a fun-loving character who performs tricks and stunts, spinning and flipping through the air with agility and grace.

FUNKY WORDS

MAGICAL	ENCHANTING	MYSTERIOUS	GIGANTIC	MISCHIEVOUS
SPARKLING	DAZZLING	WHIMSICAL	PLAYFUL	INQUISITIVE
FANTASTIC	SPECTACULAR	COLOURFUL	BRAVE	GOOFY
CURIOUS	SILLY	GLOWING	WONDROUS	RADIANT
AMAZING	FRIENDLY	ZANY	BUBBLY	MARVELLOUS
GROOVY	QUIRKY	FUNKY	SPOOKY	CHEERFUL
WACKY	SWIRLY	SNAZZY	ODDBALL	ZESTY
COSMIC	JAZZY	PERCULIAR	BIZARRE	BOUNCY
OUTLANDISH	ECCENTRIC	BOISTEROUS	FANCIFUL	SPINE-TINGLING
LIVELY	MYSTICAL	MAJESTIC	GRAND	SPIRALLING
SHIMMERING	FANTASTIC	VIBRANT	COURAGEOUS	UNUSUAL
SPACEY	MUSICAL	SPIRITED	KOOKY	STRANGE

SHAPES AND OBJECTS

CIRCLE

| CLOCK FACE | BALL | COOKIE | WHEEL | BUTTON |

SQUARE

| PICTURE FRAME | BUILDING BLOCK | WINDOW | BOOK | DICE |

TRIANGLE

| PIZZA SLICE | ROOF OF HOUSE | ROAD SIGN | SAIL ON A BOAT | PIECE OF CHEESE |

RECTANGLE

| DOOR | TV SCREEN | TABLE TOP | RUG | PICTURE BOOK |

OVAL

| EGG | RUGBY BALL | BALLOON | AVOCADO | BAR OF SOAP |

STAR

| STARFRUIT | SHERIFF'S BADGE | STAR ON A FLAG | COOKIE CUTTER | STICKER |

COLOURS AND OBJECTS

RED

| FIRE TRUCK | CHERRY | STOP SIGN | LIPSTICK | HEART |

ORANGE

| PUMPKIN | CARROT | GOLDFISH | SUNSET | APRICOT |

YELLOW

| LEMON | BANANA | CORN | RUBBER DUCK | SPONGE |

GREEN

| GRASS | FROG | LIME | PEAS | TURTLE |

BLUE

| OCEAN | SKY | ICE | BLUEBELL | WHALE |

INDIGO

| JEANS | EGG PLANT | SAPPHIRE | BLUEBERRY | INK |

VIOLET

| GRAPES | PLUM | LAVENDER | ORCHID | AMETHYST |

IDEAS FOR STORIES FROM QUESTIONS AND ANSWERS

WHO'S IN THE FOREST?

"Who's rustling in the bushes?"	"It's the playful rabbit, hopping with glee!"
"Who's soaring through the sky?"	"It's the colourful bird, singing its sweet melody!"
"Who's hiding behind the tall trees?"	"It's the mischievous squirrel, gathering nuts for winter!"

WHAT'S THAT SOUND?

"What's that sound in the distance?"	"It's the gentle pitter-patter of raindrops falling."
"What's that noise in the attic?"	"It's the scurrying of tiny mice, looking for crumbs."
"What's that rumble underground?"	"It's the playful rumble of a passing train, on its way to new adventures!"

WHO'S ON THE FARM?

"Who's munching on the green grass?"	"It's the hungry cow, mooing softly as she eats."
"Who's rolling in the mud?"	"It's the playful pig, oinking with joy!"
"Who's pecking at the corn?"	"It's the curious chicken, clucking happily in the sunshine!"

Discover more at

hackneyandjones.com

Scan QR Code

www.ingramcontent.com/pod-product-compliance
Lightning Source LLC
Chambersburg PA
CBHW080018130526
44590CB00045B/3450